What Is Economics?

To my father,
Robert J. Eggert

WHAT IS ECONOMICS?

Revised Edition

Jim Eggert

William Kaufmann, Inc.
Los Altos, California

Cartoons by Robert Cavey
Photographs by Jim Eggert and Rick Graefe

Parts of this book were previously published in *What Is
Economics?* (First Edition) and *Invitation to Economics.*

10 9 8 7 6 5 4 3 2 1

Library of Congress Cataloging in Publication Data

Eggert, Jim, 1943–
   What is economics?

   Bibliography: p.
   Includes index.
   1. Economics.   I. Title
HB171.5.E464 1987   330   86–27297
ISBN 0–86576–104–3

PREFACE

The purpose of this book is simple: it is designed to stimulate your curiosity about a very interesting and important subject—economics. Time after time, people have asked me, "What exactly *is* economics?" In this book I have attempted to answer that question.

I have tried to write *What Is Economics?* clearly and directly, using many examples from everyday life to help beginners in the subject gain an easier understanding. Although most of the major principles and issues are covered in these pages, this is obviously not an encyclopedic, detailed textbook. Rather, I hope you will regard it as an inviting narrative of the basic ideas of economics.*

What Is Economics? can be used by itself, or with a larger textbook, in formal courses, or it can be read profitably by those who do not have the opportunity to take a course in economics. Of course, the more educational resources at your disposal (including teachers!) the better will be the balance of the ideas you are exposed to and the deeper will be your understanding of the entire subject.

I appreciate the opportunity my publisher has given me to prepare a new edition of this book. Revising and rewriting some of the text, updating it throughout, and adding new chapters on international trade has been a challenging, instructive, and satisfying experience for me. I trust that previous users of the earlier edition will find the book improved throughout. To my wife Pat, my father Bob Eggert, and to Dave Liu, Lou Tokle, and many other readers whose comments have helped make this a better book, I offer warm thanks. Special words of thanks are also due to James Pinto, who not only made many helpful editorial suggestions but also prepared the Student Study Guide that accompanies this book.

---

*For a more extensive treatment that includes additional chapters on microeconomics, I refer interested readers to my 1984 book, *Invitation To Economics*, also published by William Kaufmann, Inc.

Finally, I owe thanks to cartoonist Bob Cavey, whose contributions are apparent throughout the book, and—not least—to all of my own "econ" students over the years whose indirect contributions of most importance are enormous and would be difficult to measure.

Jim Eggert
University of Wisconsin-Stout
Menomonie, Wisconsin

Publishers note: Throughout rest of this text, the numbered footnotes will be found at the end of the book, pp 195–198.

CONTENTS

The first woman on earth, according to Greek mythology, was Pandora. She was endowed by the gods with every charm, including curiosity. When the god, Zeus, sent her to Epimetheus, brother of Prometheus, as a wife, he sent a box with her but forbade her to open it. Prometheus warned Pandora against disobeying Zeus, but with her husband's approval, she opened the box. Thus Pandora let out the troubles (including economics) that have afflicted mankind ever since. But something very important remained in the box: HOPE. And it is the hope of the author and the publisher of *What is Economics?* that this little book will help make your study of economics memorable, entertaining and enlightening.

Chapter 1

What Is Economics?

What Is Economics?

Unfortunately, there is no single or simple answer to this question. In the most basic sense, economics is the study of how individuals or communities survive (and reproduce) using scarce resources. Indeed, this definition could apply to all life-forms as they pursue their successful evolution over time. Using this approach, we might, for example, examine "bumblebee economics," "bluebird economics," or the complex interrelationships of a biological community such as a prairie or rain forest.[1]

Of course, most of our emphasis in this book will be on human societies. Here economics originally meant *household management*. Still, the "economic problem" is the same; i.e., how to best use our scarce resources. Household resources might include a family's money, time, working and living space and so forth. Of course our human objectives are much more complicated than simple survival. People have a wide variety of economic desires which include, among other things, general comfort, financial security, interesting diversions, recreational pursuits, health and longevity. In fact for most households or individuals, the economic wants appear for all practical purposes to be *unlimited*.

We are also different from other animals in that we are able to make *deliberate choices* as to how our limited resources will be used. Thus, a basic definition of economics might go something like this: *Economics is the study of how an individual or household chooses to use limited resources to best meet their unlimited wants.*

Let us now extend our view from the household economy to the national economy. The basic economic problem is the same:

the nation's resources are limited. Our material demands, however, tend to be unlimited, and the nation must learn how to best organize its resources to satisfy its material wants. Unwise use of resources—whether by consumers, businesses, or governments—can bring about unfortunate results such as unemployment, inflation, poverty, and (in extreme cases) hunger or starvation. The study of economics can help us understand how we might avoid such mismanagement of these national resources.

National Resources

What exactly then are our national economic resources? The first and primary resource is *labor*. This includes the millions of men and women in the U.S. labor force: the doctor, the farmer, the butcher, the assembly line worker, and so forth. Labor is thus the *human* element within the production process.

Next is *land*. America's land resources include every natural resource above, on, and below the soil. Air is a land resource, as is crop land. The mineral ores and petroleum in the crust of the earth are also land resources. These resources are distinguished by the fact that man cannot make more of them. The earth has only so much topsoil and so much oil. Once the topsoil has been destroyed[2] and the oil burned up, they will be gone forever.

The third major resource is *capital*. Many people think that capital means money; you often hear someone say "I need to raise so much capital for my new project." What is actually being referred to is financial capital. To the economist, capital means the physical tools that aid the worker in production. In other words, capital goods are man-made, can be reproduced or replaced, and tend to increase the productivity of labor. What are some examples of capital goods? The typewriter that I use is a capital good. It is a tool that increases my output; it's man-made (unlike land resources); and, once it wears out, I can replace it. The pen that you wrote your last check with is a capital good and so is the car that gets you to work. In fact, all machinery, tools, buildings, plants, and equipment are capital resources. (You can see now that there is much more to the meaning of capital than just plain money.) Capital goods are thus very important in determining the nation's level of wealth and economic growth.

Finally, we come to that elusive resource called *management.* The manager is quite special in our economy; it is he or she who coordinates and organizes all the other resources in order to produce and market the products and services that people want, thereby creating a profit. In the old days, the manager was called an entrepreneur; we think, for example, of Henry Ford or Andrew Carnegie as large-scale managers personifying this scarce resource. Perhaps the days of the great "wheeling-dealing" entrepreneurs are over, but whether you are talking about the bakery down the street or General Motors, some one person or group of people must still coordinate resources to produce saleable products and services.

Asking Questions, Making Choices

Thus, labor, land, capital, and management are the four major resources available to our economy to produce goods and services that people need and want.

To define a working economic system, however, we must ask further questions; for example, *How does an economic system determine what will be produced?* What will our economic output consist of, and who will determine its composition? Will our economy produce bombs and tanks or hospitals and homes? Small cars, large cars, or bikes and trains? Gas, oil, or solar heat? Who or what will decide for us? Of course, different economic systems will provide different answers to these questions. The Soviet Union or communist China determines what will be produced in a manner somewhat different from that of the United States or Brazil.

In addition, there are other important questions to ask, such as, *How does the economic system decide who gets the output?* Why are incomes, goods, and services distributed the way they are? Throughout U.S. history, dividing up the economic pie has always been a very controversial question. Will our economic system give a majority of the output to a few "super rich" families, will it try to divide the pie up more equally, or will it fall somewhere in between? Uneven distribution of incomes and wealth is often a result of differences in education, intelligence, skills, work habits, monopoly power, geography, family background, luck, and political or social savvy. More equal incomes, on the other hand, usually come about through government policies such as minimum-wage laws, progressive taxation, subsidized education, and welfare assistance.

And finally, there is the question, *How will these goods be produced?* At first glance, the answer might seem to be a purely technical one. Building an automobile, for example, is a problem for the engineer. And yet we know there are really many ways to produce a finished automobile. Ideally we want to build efficiently, using abundant, low-cost resources in place of scarce, high-cost resources. Assembling that car one way in preference to another returns us to the question of allocating resources. Choosing the correct techniques for production (conserving the scarce resources and using the abundant) is thus as much an economic problem as it is a technical or engineering problem. Economics is therefore the science (or art) of making choices—choosing the best way to organize our limited resources in order to meet our material needs.

Finding Answers

The method by which an economic system answers these questions varies from time to time and from country to country. Economist Robert Heilbroner in his book, *The Making of Economic Society*, explains that there are in fact three basic systems for organizing economic resources.

The first is called *tradition*. The decision makers in a traditional system answer these questions by saying, "We will organize our economy the way we have always organized it," i.e., by age-old patterns determined by a complex culture that had evolved over thousands of years. Tools and houses are constructed as they were always constructed. Junior goes into the same trade as his father. Output is allocated by custom, with few changes over the years and only with minute trial-and-error improvements over the centuries; it is, in short predictable, predetermined and static.

Economics by tradition certainly has some advantages: There may be less conflict, and there are probably few expectations that can't be met. But it is likely to be a system offering a relatively low standard of living—at least as we would define it. If you feel that having more choices moves you closer to the good life, then the traditional economic system is probably not for you.

Yet we certainly have elements of tradition in our so-called "modern economy." For example, my own father is an economist, and he was once a teacher. Many instructors still use a lecture method that dates back to Plato in ancient Greece, even though some critics think that the lecture technique should have been dropped with the invention of the printing press. Whether the critics are correct or not, contemporary education certainly adheres to very traditional methods of performance. Women, too, have become more aware of the extent to which their lives are determined by social and economic tradition.[3] By discriminating on the basis of sex and thus eliminating a large proportion of our population from competing for highly productive and professional jobs, our economy has lost a potentially vast economic force. You can probably think of many more examples of how tradition subtly weaves in and out of our supposedly "modern" economy.

The second way to solve the economic problem is with a *command system*. A command system is characterized by the allocation of resources, incomes, prices, etc., by a centralized authority; in other words, a dictatorship. The command system invites no questions—either you follow orders or you take the consequences. This system is often the offspring of a despotic political system; they frequently go hand in hand. The economy of the Soviet Union is a good example.

European democratic socialists believe, however, that we can have a planned, state-directed economy without the terror. The combination appears to be difficult, and yet democratic state planning has been approximated in Scandinavia, Japan, and a few eastern European countries. The U.S. economy too has some elements of economic command. Our military services, for example, work on this principle, as does the government allocation of goods during wartime. When price-wage controls are in effect, we have a perfect example of government command. Furthermore, almost all government laws on economic affairs (including our tax system) constitute direction from above. By and large, however, our private enterprise system cannot really be called either command or traditional.

What we have in the United States is a *market economy*. The market system is a relatively recent phenomenon. Instead of using force to get things done (as in the command system), the market system motivates people by offering economic rewards within a process of exchange. Instead of government direction, decisions on resource use are made by millions of independent individuals and institutions attempting to do what is best for themselves or their businesses. Here the economic mule moves by carrot instead of stick. The U.S. economy is indeed a system of carrots.

If the command system is centralized, the market system is decentralized. A market economy churns out prices in countless markets of supply and demand, and these prices in turn act as guidelines in a new round of economic decisions; it is a competitive, interdependent, and self-regulating system. If you and I were not so accustomed to such an arrangement, we might find it somewhat strange, as we see in Heilbroner's little scenario:

> . . . assume for a moment that we could act as economic advisors to a society which had not yet decided on its mode of economic organization. . . .. We could imagine the leaders of such a nation saying, "We have always experienced a highly tradition-bound way of life. Our men hunt and cultivate the fields and perform their tasks as they are brought up to do by the force of example and the instruction of their elders. We know, too, something of what can be done by economic command. We are prepared, if necessary to sign an edict making it compulsory for many of our men to work on community projects for our national development. Tell us, is there any other way we can organize our society so that it will function successfully—or better yet, more successfully?"
>
> Suppose we answered, "yes, there is another way. Organize your society along the lines of a market economy."
>
> "Very well," say the leaders. "What do we then tell the people to do? How do we assign them to their various tasks?"
>
> "That's the very point," we answer. "In a market economy no one is assigned to any task. The very idea of market society is that each person is allowed to decide for himself what to do."
>
> There is consternation among the leaders. "You mean there is no assignment of some men to mining and others to cattle raising? . . . What happens if no one volunteers to go into the mines, or if no one offers himself as a railway engineer?"[4]

The leaders argue on and on, unable to fully comprehend what motivates people in a market system—despite the explanation that it is in everyone's self-interest (more money, profits, etc.) to do whatever is necessary. Finally, the African representatives end the discussion saying, "We thought you had in mind a serious proposal. But what you suggest is madness," and then with great dignity they take their leave.

Economic Sacrifices

Another way of looking at economics is to examine sacrifices. Economists call these *opportunity costs*. What exactly do they mean?

Let's say that you have spent half an hour reading this chapter. By spending this time reading, you have given up doing something else. In all likelihood you have given up a number of activities you would have enjoyed. Thus, when you use up one of your resources (an hour of time, a dollar, etc.) the cost to you is really the opportunities that you have forfeited. That hour is gone forever and so are the alternative activities you might have enjoyed. Sometimes we hear the question, "If you had your life to live over, would you do it any differently?" If you answer yes, then you are referring indirectly to your opportunity cost.

Although the above explanation of opportunity cost is somewhat philosophical, the economic concept is much the same. Economists look at the sacrifices that must be made when the economic resources of land, labor, capital, and management are used. If, for example, we commit our resources to producing 10 million automobiles, then these resources cannot be used for alternative goods and services such as housing or mass transit. Thus, the economist (unlike the business person) is not only interested in monetary costs but also in the question of what is going to be sacrificed when resources are put to use.

The idea of looking at economic costs as sacrifices can be seen quite dramatically in Figure 1–1.

Look, for example, at point A. We can assume that A represents an economy much like our own, i.e., it has directed most of its total resources toward the production of "butter" (private consumer goods) and comparatively fewer resources toward "guns" (military expenditures). As you move away from zero on either the "guns" or "butter" line, you are producing more and more of that good. Thus, point B represents a country that has chosen to produce more military goods than consumer goods (such as the United States during World War II). Given the fact that a country has only

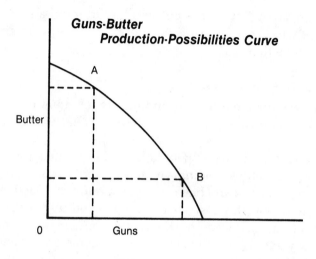

Figure 1-1

so many total resources, they are forced to choose some mix on the line between guns and butter. This line or curve is called the *production-possibilities curve.*

Our production-possibilities curve thus represents all the various choices open to society regarding consumer or military production. With our limited resources we may favor butter (A) or guns (B), but note that we cannot have a large amount of both goods—there are simply not enough total resources! In fact, to move from point A to point B means that the production of guns *must be sacrificed* to get more butter. Putting the opportunity cost idea slightly different, economists sometimes say, "There is no such thing as a free lunch!"

The true cost (opportunity cost) is, therefore, the measure of what is sacrificed. Thus we might view the true economic cost of a war as all the good things that could have been produced or accomplished instead. Or, the true cost of having so many cars is that the resources are not available to produce mass transit systems (see Figure 1–3).

Let's now take a look at another production-possibilities curve, (see Figure 1–2) this time representing a less developed country like China.

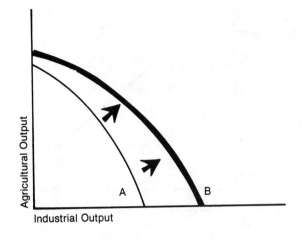

Figure 1-2

Curve A represents China at an early stage of development, with more agricultural potential than industrial potential. However, an expanding production curve such as line B represents China after economic growth. The kind of economic growth that China chose in this example tended to favor industrial output over agricultural output. This is a typical pattern for economic development throughout the world.

Finally, there is an additional piece of information we can gather by examining a production-possibilities curve. Take a look at Figure 1–3.

Assume for a moment that the United States is producing a lot of cars and few mass transit systems; the country is therefore operating at point A. Suppose, though, that we decide to put more resources into mass transit and move down the curve a little way from A to A⁺. Note how much additional mass transit there is in relation to the relatively small amount of sacrificed cars. If, however, we are producing a lot in mass transit (point B) and want even more, we gain the same amount as before when we move to B⁺. Note the difference in the real cost of obtaining that extra mass transit; the number of sacrificed automobiles is much larger. We might say, then, that as we move to higher levels of mass transit,

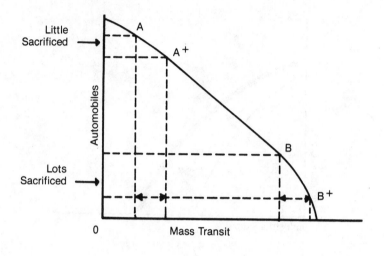

Figure 1-3

the opportunity cost of squeezing out yet *more* mass transit be-comes greater and greater as more and more cars have to be sacri-ficed. Obviously when a country is producing almost all mass tran-sit, there are few interchangeable resources left to make the switch to even more mass transit; the sacrifice (or cost), therefore, must be very high to gain these additional trains, buses, etc. Econo-mists call this phenomenon *the law of increasing costs.*

The Economist's Concerns

Let's return to our original question: What is economics? We might answer this question by simply saying that economics is "what economists study." Most economists, in fact, are not much con-cerned with broad generalizations such as "studying how to best allocate resources to meet our unlimited wants." They are more in-terested in the specific economic problems of society, such as un-employment, inflation, balance of payments, economic stagnation, and pollution. We could then say that economics is the study of how we solve economic problems.

Alternatively, we could view economics as the study of goals, i.e., how we move closer to specific economic objectives. These economic goals are more or less universal; i.e., most countries—capitalistic, socialistic, and communistic—are striving to achieve them.

The primary economic goal that seems to be universally desired is a decent material standard of living for all citizens, and thus much of our economic activity contributes toward this goal. But what exactly are the steps or intermediate goals that lead to such a "successful economy"?

The first of these objectives is *full employment*. Nations would like to see all, or nearly all, of their available resources being used. Men and women out of work or machines and factories idle can result in great economic suffering and social instability. It is foolish to have unused resources when there are the means to correct the situation. How we move an economy toward full employment will be explored later in the text.

The second goal of an economic system is *price stability*. Rapid price increases—or what is commonly called *inflation*—have the undesirable effect of grossly distorting income distribution. The victims include people on fixed incomes, savers, and lenders. While these groups lose, others win including borrowers and speculators. At best, mild inflation is merely irritating, if it is accompanied by full employment. At its worst, however, inflation invites panic buying and can lead to the eventual collapse of a monetary system.

Note the conflicts that arise in pursuing these various economic goals, such as with price stability and full employment. For example, when there is high-unemployment, there is frequently lower inflation, and if there is high inflation, almost everyone is working. Thus as we struggle to achieve one economic objective, we sometimes lose our grip on another.

The third goal is *growth*. There are respected critics who argue that the United States is presently overdeveloped and who believe that we would benefit by not adding any more to our economic affluence. And yet, most Americans, and most other people in the world, seem to desire higher and higher levels of output and consumption. We feel concerned when the total economic output fails to rise; if output drops, alarms are sounded throughout government and business. Furthermore, in the poorest two thirds of the world, a lack of economic growth means hunger and possible starvation.

Fourth, we all desire a *quality environment*. The mounting evidence of the massive pollution problems that face this small planet compels economists to regard the environment as a major economic issue. But again note the potential conflicts that arise in pursuing these various economic goals. For example, strong enforcement of antipollution laws may well slow down economic growth. "Everything has a price," says one man jokingly to another in a newspaper cartoon. "To get a high standard of living we have to reduce the quality of life."

A fifth goal of an economic society is to move toward a *fair distribution of income*. This does not mean, however, an absolutely equal distribution; perfect equality would be unrealistic and probably undesirable for it would destroy healthy economic incentives. On the other hand, most economists would agree that a system which allows a large number of its citizens to live in terrible poverty while others enjoy immense wealth is certainly unfair. What then can we do about a grossly unequal system?

Generally accepted methods of moving toward a more equal distribution of income include government taxation and redistribution of income (welfare, food stamps, Medicare, etc.) and also the enforcement of equal opportunity in education and job procurement. If the government became, as some have suggested, "the employer of last resort," then it would have even greater impact in this area. Although some people disapprove of government intervention, the policies and programs mentioned above are at least some of the ways we can break down the natural, social, and institutional inequalities that operate in all societies.

The last goal is *economic freedom*. Like our goal of fair income distribution, economic freedom is sometimes difficult to define precisely. To many Americans, economic freedom will thrive in a decentralized, free enterprise system. This includes freedom for the workers to choose occupations commensurate with their skills and experience. By this definition, twentieth century America may be one of the "freest" economies in the world. Yet the critic might ask what meaning economic freedom has for a consumer without income. Indeed, what occupational freedom does an unskilled person have in a high unemployment area? In fact, what real freedom of enterprise would you or I have if we were to attempt to compete with IT&T, Proctor and Gamble, or the Ford Motor Company? The ideal of economic freedom is thus diluted by income inequalities, by barriers imposed by large, concentrated industries, and also by restrictive policies and regulations of government. But compare the United States with other countries, and it's clear that the United States would score quite high in meeting this objective.

You might take a moment now and think about these six goals in relationship to yourself; how does the nation's economic performance—in terms of freedom, price stability, employment, growth, fairness, and the environment—affect *you?* Does the national economy help or perhaps hinder your effort to create your own "successful economy?"

Thus, whether we like it or not, we are all connected to the larger economic system. It is now time to take a more intimate look at some of the characteristics and inner workings of that larger system: our own U.S. economy.

Chapter 2

THE U.S. ECONOMY

What is the nation's economy like? What makes it tick? Suppose a foreigner asked you to describe your economic system. What would you say?

We learned in Chapter 1 that our economic system is basically a market economy. Let's now amplify this important idea. A pure market economy is self-regulated, interdependent, and competitive. Self-regulation takes place when supply and demand operate for every good and service that has economic value. There is a market for welders and secretaries, for wheat and bread, for toothpicks and plows. Each of these markets is constantly interacting with hundreds of others. This process churns out prices, and these prices in turn modify other markets and influence economic decisions. Let's look at an illustration.

We will begin by assuming that there is a shortage of milk, and, as a consequence, the price of milk goes up. In a market economy, buyers and sellers note this signal (high milk prices) and then respond in various ways. First, the existing dairy farmers demand more cows and farm land so that they can expand their operations and increase their profits. Soon, higher profits in milk production begin to attract more farmers into the dairy industry.

This growing number of farmers will now be demanding more milking machines and silos. Stainless steel for milking machines and cement for silos will be diverted into farming and away from other industries. Milking machine manufacturers, for example, will try to outbid steel-pipe manufacturers for the available steel. Plumbers now find that steel pipes are simply priced too high. They discover that low-cost plastic pipes can do the job almost as well. Suddenly the plastic industry has a need for new people and raw materials: chemists and petroleum. The many readjustments—both large and small—that could take place because of a milk price increase are almost endless. Note that in this example no economic dictatorship tells people what to do; everything takes place automatically in response to price signals in the marketplace.

In reality, our neat system of supply and demand is often not allowed to regulate itself. The government, reacting to special economic interest groups, is often the culprit. For example, when the federal government imposes price-wage controls, we find that prices are no longer flexible. If prices are not allowed to move upward or downward, the signals are thwarted. Shortages and black markets develop where the demand for certain products is great. We can see something similar happening when city governments impose rent controls. Rents that are artificially low create greater quantity demanded than is supplied, leaving many frustrated demanders. Other examples of governmental market regulation include farm subsidies, the setting of minimum wage laws, and tariffs. Each time the government interferes with the free movement of prices, market efficiency is usually reduced.

Specialization

Our economy can also be described as *specialized*. All of us specialize. You may specialize in programming computers, making handmade furniture, fixing cars, or tightening a bolt on an automobile assembly line. If we did not specialize, many of us would be forced to become self-sufficient—like the original settlers of the American frontier—and we would undoubtedly undergo a reduced standard of living.

Why does output increase when workers specialize? Some people, of course, simply have natural abilities in some specialties. Also, the more we work at our particular job, the faster and generally more efficient we become. We learn the shortcuts and how to use the special tools that increase our productivity. The assembly line operation is a good example of how specialization and division of labor can create greater output than a system of nonspecialized workers.

Specialization can be worthwhile even when an individual has superior skills in several areas. For example, Jim is a good plumber, but he is also a good auto mechanic. Bob is a plumber and an auto mechanic as well. Bob, however, is almost a genius at fixing cars, whereas Jim is just average. As plumbers their skills are about equal, but Bob is a little better here too. Even though Bob has an *absolute advantage* in both skills, he has a *comparative advantage only* in auto mechanics; that is, his advantage is bigger than Jim's in mechanics rather than plumbing. Jim is not as good in either skill, but his disadvantage is smaller in plumbing. We therefore say Jim has his comparative advantage in plumbing. If they lived in a town that had room for only one plumber and one auto mechanic, the economy would be more productive if Bob stayed with auto mechanics and Jim concentrated on plumbing. In short, specialization will bring about higher output in almost all situations.

Some economists feel, however, that we are overspecialized despite the gains from comparative advantage. One drawback of specialization is that we become highly dependent on our specialists. What would happen if the truck drivers and railway workers—only about 1 percent of the labor force—went on strike at the same time? Our economy would be paralyzed within a week. If the strike lasted a month, we might have starvation and mass panic. The slender threads of economic interdependence can easily be broken in a complex economy such as ours. There is also some evidence that overspecialization on the assembly line and in menial jobs takes its psychological toll:

> The man whose whole life is spent in performing simple operations which the effects to are, perhaps, always the same, or very nearly the same, has no occasion to exert his understanding or to exercise his invention . . . He naturally loses, therefore, the habit of such exertion and generally becomes as stupid and ignorant as it is possible for a human creature to become.

Adam Smith wrote this in his book, *Inquiry into the Nature and Causes of the Wealth of Nations* in 1776. Even today we see some people rebelling against overspecialization. It is not uncommon to read about individuals or families moving from the cities into the country to set up "new homesteads" where they can operate their semi-self-sufficient farms with little specialization. Often they build their own homes, make their own clothes, and grow much of their food, as most of our nation's farmers did generations ago. Even

though their material standard of living is usually lower than average, they take great pride in their work and seem quite happy with their newly found independence.[5]

Finally, there is evidence that many people—even with specialized jobs—would like to rely less on the services of others. Gardening, for example, is on the increase, as is doing one's own auto maintenance; in addition, "do-it-yourself" remodeling has always been popular in this country. This trend seems to defy the laws of comparative advantage and specialization. Still, by and large, we remain primarily specialists operating within a very specialized and interdependent American economy.

Self-interest

If much of our high productivity and efficiency in the U.S. economy comes from specialization and division of labor, the motivation to do all this work comes from self-interest. Why do some people go into hot, dirty mines or get up early on a cold winter morning to work on an outdoor construction site? Why does the barber cheerfully cut your hair even when he isn't feeling so hot? Why does GM make Chevrolets? Why do companies go to all the trouble of making safety pins to help you diaper your baby? There is no economic commander in chief telling them what to do, and they don't do it because of tradition. They perform their job *because it is in their own self-interest to do so.* Economists call this self-interest *income maximization,* others call it "just trying to make a living." Whatever it's called, it is the motor of our capitalist economic system. Things get done because each individual group or institution is constantly trying to enlarge its base of income, consumption, or profit.

The self-interest of businesses is to maximize profits. The self-interest of workers is to maximize their income. Finally, the self-interest of consumers is to maximize their material satisfactions from limited incomes. Surprisingly enough, in this very "self-centered" economic turmoil, the society as a whole benefits! This is what Adam Smith called the *invisible hand.* In *Wealth of Nations* he said that each individual (or business) pursuing his own interest is "led by an invisible hand to promote the end which was not part of his intention."

It was not the intention of the safety pin company to make it easier for parents to diaper their babies. Their purpose was to make a profit. The company therefore had to make something society wanted. This is where the safety pins came in. If the company did not make a product society wanted, it would be eliminated by the laws of economics. You might recall an ad from the Sun Oil Company; it had a refreshing honesty about it:

> These days, I need all the friends I can get. This is a tough business I'm in. You really have to hustle to make a buck. And right now I need the bucks. I'm due for a new wrecker. A new car. And my wife's screaming for an avocado refrigerator. That's why, when you drive into my station, I'm going to come out smiling. I'm going to wash your front window. Your back window. Now to be honest, I'm not really crazy about having to work this hard, but I need that new wrecker, the new car, and like my wife says, what's an avocado kitchen without an avocado refrigerator? Try me, I can be very friendly.

Of course, not everyone is interested in maximizing their income. Henry David Thoreau once said, "None can be an impartial or wise observer of human life but from the vantage ground of what we should call voluntary poverty." And in James Park's thought-provoking article, "Four Reasons for Voluntary Poverty,"[6] Park explains that income maximization can lead to exploitation, pollution, compromises on personal freedom, and a tacit support of militarism (through taxes). Readers will have to decide for themselves whether voluntary poverty is a desirable path to follow. It seems safe to say, however, that if a majority of workers and businesses renounced income and profit maximization, the U.S. economic system would be radically different from what it is today.

Private Ownership

Another notable characteristic of the American economy is *private ownership*. If we were living under a socialistic instead of a capitalistic system, then the means of production—the businesses, factories, capital, and other resources—would be largely publicly owned.

The debate over socialism versus capitalism has been going on for years. Unfortunately, opinions are too often based on emotion rather than on factual information. Many people, for example, are convinced that socialism implies a political system that is totalitarian, ruthless, and nonlibertarian. The truth is that political despotism can thrive in a capitalist state (South Africa, Brazil) as well as in a socialist one (U.S.S.R., Cuba). Again, the major difference between the two systems is the following: socialism means that businesses are owned and controlled by the public, whereas capitalism implies that businesses are owned and controlled privately. To say much more is to confuse the issue.

Consider now the term "communism." How does it differ from capitalism and socialism? Karl Marx defined communism as a system where the production-distribution philosophy was, "From each according to his ability, to each according to his need." Surprisingly, our most "communistic" institution is the family. In most conventional family setups members receive an approximately equal distribution of goals and services. Consumption is based on "need" instead of productive effort (an infant, for example, doesn't work for its formula). Pure communism has been approximated by a few comparatively small groups (the Shakers and some North American Indian communities, for example), but on a national scale it doesn't appear to be as practical as the more common socialistic or capitalistic economies.

Competition

Another characteristic of the U.S. economy is *competition*. Perhaps no other quality of American capitalism draws as much praise.

Proponents of the capitalist system say that competition allows the most intelligent and skillful to prevail in a "dog eat-dog" battle for survival. This is a virtue, they say, because in a system where only the fittest and strongest come out on top, the economic organization itself will remain strong and healthy. Producers must make a cheaper, better product than their rivals, or they will find themselves out of business. A competitive economy is like a grand-scale pro football game where, according to the late Green Bay Packer Coach Vince Lombardi, "Winning isn't everything, it's the only thing." It should be noted that some people feel this kind of "competition" may be unhealthy. Educator George Leonard, for example, writes:

> The . . . argument for hot competition all the way down to nursery school is that competition makes winners. The argument is, at best, half true. It makes nonwinners, too—generally more nonwinners

than winners. And a number of studies indicate that losing can become a lifelong habit.

What is perhaps even more interesting is a businessman's reaction to the suggestion that this kind of competition creates more problems than it solves. Leonard continues:

> I once spoke to a group of top ranking industrialists in a seminar session and argued that hot competition is far from inevitable in the future. As my argument developed I noticed a look of real anxiety on some of the faces around me. One industrialist finally spoke up, "If there is to be no competition, then what will life be all about?" We would probably be appalled to discover how many people in this culture have no notion of accomplishment for its own sake and define their own existence solely in terms of how many other people they can beat out.[7]

To beat out your opponent and to build a better product than your rival are thus common ways of defining competition. Economists, however, define it somewhat differently. A good example of a competitive industry in the United States is farming, with tens of thousands of producers who usually don't care about what the other producers are doing! In pure competition there are in fact *no differences* between the sellers' products. For example, grade A milk is generally the same throughout the industry. We never see advertisements claiming that Farmer Jones' milk is better than Farmer Brown's. Another characteristic of competition is that no seller is big enough to set prices or to control the market. A competitive industry is the *least concentrated* of all industries. (In contrast, a monopoly is the most concentrated.)

Obviously, to be a producer in a truly competitive industry is to operate at a disadvantage. For example, the farmer's inability to control prices and their low rate of return on investment are problems that have plagued U.S. agriculture for a long time. Even though competition may mean "hard times" for sellers it usually gives consumers the lowest possible price. Furthermore, the more sellers, the more potential choice for the buyer. Competition is therefore a kind of "insurance policy" against getting ripped off.

Since real competition can be threatening to businesses, we see all kinds of efforts to do away with it. Sellers can sometimes lessen competition by eliminating other sellers; by erecting barriers so that new firms have a difficult time entering; and, finally, by making products slightly different from other sellers in the industry. Keep in mind that even though a decentralized competitive market is a traditional American "ideal," it is a rare sight on our economic landscape.

To summarize, we can say that industry is purely competitive if it has the following characteristics:

- A large number of sellers of the same product
- No single seller with any control over price
- Easy entry into the industry
- Low profits in the long run
- No rivalry among sellers

Monopolies

Let's look now at the other extreme. If competition allows consumers the widest potential choice, a monopoly market structure gives the consumer the least choice. The monopoly seller has total control over his economic kingdom. If you are a consumer and want the goods, you must buy from him. He is, in short, a "one-firm industry."

Are there any good examples of monopolies in the United States? Well, your local telephone company has an effective monopoly on local telephone service. The government, too, holds a legal monopoly on first-class mail. The companies that sell you electricity and natural gas are also monopolies. We call them *natural monopolies* because the market is too small to accommodate more than one seller. If, for example, your local utility already has electric power lines leading to your home, it would obviously be inefficient (and also very costly) for another firm to do the same. We therefore tolerate natural monopolies. You might wonder how the consumer is protected from profit-maximizing utilities. The answer is by government regulation. Although their monopolies are legally protected, their prices and rates are subject to review by public commissions.

There are other monopolies, however, that operate without any restrictions. Imagine a small town with just one drug store or only one dentist. We call this kind of market a *regional monopoly*. We can't say they are pure monopolies because there may be another drug store twenty miles away. Yet for the retired residents of that town or for those without transportation, the one drug store becomes an effective monopoly operating without any competitive or regulatory restraints. Here, the buyer is at the mercy of the seller. Did you ever have a nightmare where your car broke down in the middle of nowhere, and you discover there is just one garage within fifty miles? You can just see the owner of the garage rubbing his hands together as his tow truck brings your car in. Unregulated monopolies can be bad news!

We can also see monopolistic behavior among the big industrialists. American Tobacco, Standard Oil, and Alcoa Aluminum were at one time considered monopolies. Others, such as General Electric and Westinghouse, simply conspired during the late 1950s to set prices on certain products and behaved as if they were a single monopoly. This arrangement is called a *cartel*.

However it occurs, such monopolistic behavior is illegal under the Sherman Antitrust Act of 1890. Section 2 reads:

> Every person who shall monopolize, or attempt to monopolize, or combine or conspire with any person or persons . . . shall be deemed guilty of a misdemeanor . . . .

The antitrust laws were written in an attempt to reverse the natural tendency for industries to become more concentrated. In capitalism, the big often get bigger; and if one firm begins to dominate a market, there is a natural tendency for that firm to attempt to eliminate (or merge with) rivals.

Let's now review the conditions for a monopoly:

- Only one seller (i.e., one choice for the consumer)
- No close substitutes for the product the monopolist sells
- Great barriers of entry into the industry
- Usually higher prices than in a competitive market

There is one industry that fits all these conditions and yet is not ordinarily considered a monopoly: the public school system. Some economists point out that the public school monopoly contains all the undesirable features of an industrial monopoly, i.e., a no-choice situation, high costs, lack of innovation, and so forth. Not only do consumers have no alternative, they *must* also "consume" the "product" whether they want to or not. Not to do so means prison or detention under the compulsory-attendance laws. To make things more difficult, a child often cannot get out of going to school even if he or she knows the required material. Would less compulsion and more choice make for a better system? Many educators and economists think that some alternative system is worth a try.

Milton Friedman, for one, has suggested a *voucher* system where parents would be allowed to choose the kind of schooling they would like for their children.[8] It would be something like the GI Bill for veterans. (No one, for example, tells a student on the GI Bill that he must go to a military academy. The student can go to any accredited school.) Under Friedman's system, you might choose to use your educational vouchers for a public school, a private school, or even an apprenticeship. "Voluntary organizations—ranging from vegetarians to Boy Scouts to the YMCA—could set up schools and try to attract customers." Indeed, the voucher system is an interesting proposal; but whether it would bring about a new age in American education or create new kinds of problems, we won't know until we try it in some form or another.

Oligopolies

We have not yet mentioned the most prevalent type of industrial structure in the American economy. It's not competition, and it's not monopoly. Economists call this type of industry an *oligopoly*, an industry dominated by a few firms. Think of almost everything we buy—automobiles, steel, aluminum, processed food, appliances, gasoline, etc. The companies that dominate each of these industries can often be counted on one hand.

Other major characteristics of an oligopoly-type industry include:

- Emphasis on *nonprice competition* (advertising, product differentiation, styling, service, etc.)

- *Price leadership* usually by the largest firm
- Great difficulty (because of *barriers of entry*) for newcomers to compete with established firms.
- *Limited choice* for buyers between a few suppliers

Look carefully at the pyramid (see Figure 2–1) to see how oligopoly fits between competition and monopoly in respect to market concentration. The oligopoly industries are quite concentrated. Indeed, they are closer to the monopoly end of the spectrum than to pure competition.

LEVELS OF CONCENTRATION

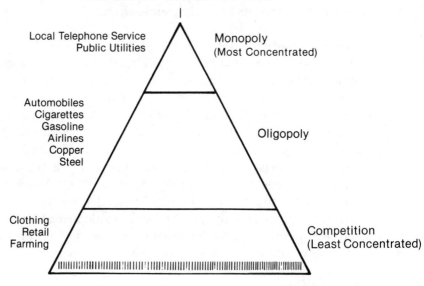

Local Telephone Service
Public Utilities

Monopoly
(Most Concentrated)

Automobiles
Cigarettes
Gasoline
Airlines
Copper
Steel

Oligopoly

Clothing
Retail
Farming

Competition
(Least Concentrated)

Figure 2-1

One of the major features of the oligopoly is *entry barriers*. What if you decided to start a rival company in the automobile industry? What difficulties would you encounter? For one thing, you would need millions and millions of dollars just to build one assembly plant, and even if you built it, you would still be left with a massive marketing problem. You would have to convince a large number of dealerships to handle your product. Even if you did that, why would anyone go out of his way to buy your car? They probably wouldn't, at least until you had established a name for yourself. This might take years and additional millions for advertising—and this still would not include the high cost of financing annual model changeovers. Indeed, potential investors would probably consider your undertaking doomed to failure. Even large corporations with similar products (such as farm machinery or air frames) would hesitate to plunge into such a hazardous venture. The economic barriers are simply too great.

Well, what has happened to our model of the American economy? We began by saying that it was a market economy, competitive and regulated by supply and demand. Though these concepts are still operational to some degree, we are nevertheless forced to modify some of our traditional viewpoints:

> "But aren't we now saying that most of our economy is dominated by oligopolists?"
> "Yes."
> "And didn't you say that it's very difficult for a newcomer to invade oligopoly markets because there are so many barriers?"
> "Yes."
> "Then, whatever happened to the so-called 'free enterprise ideal'?"
> "To be truthful, it's not easy to find. We do see it in local service and retail, some innovative small-scale manufacturing (such as computer software) and above all, in the supply-demand-determined industries like farming."
> "Supply and demand—can we go into that in more detail?"
> "Good idea!"

Chapter 3

SUPPLY AND DEMAND

You can hardly open up a magazine or newspaper without hearing someone refer to the idea of supply and demand: "lower (or higher) food prices are a result of the supply and demand for farm commodities . . ." "U.S. housing market depends upon the supply and demand for money" . . . "the future world energy situation can only be understood through supply and demand." I even heard a man say "economics is really nothing more than understanding supply and demand." An exaggeration? Yes, but not by much. So what does it all mean?

The Demand Curve

Let's begin with demand. To demand something means more than just having a desire for a product; it implies that you want that product *and* have the money to buy it. As an example, your effective demand for a hamburger will be made evident only when you actually go out and buy one.

Economists are also interested in how many hamburgers people demand at different prices. By observing the quantity of goods bought at a variety of prices, they can work out what is called the *demand curve*. Let's look at an example.

Suppose that the price of sweet corn is $5 a bushel. Let's say that people buy 5 bushels at that price. Then, if we lower the price to $4, we note that they will buy 10 bushels, and so forth. As we lower the price, observe how much more corn people will buy:

P($)	$5	$4	$3	$2	$1
Quantity (bu)	5	10	20	30	40

This information, in turn, can easily be graphed (see Figure 3–1).

The lower the price, the greater the quantity that is demanded. Makes sense, doesn't it? For example, when your local grocery store lowers the price on certain vegetables, more of those vegetables will usually be sold. Behind this simple economic law, however, is some fairly complicated reasoning; let's look at what's involved.

One reason people buy more when the price goes down is that regular buyers of corn now find that their *real incomes* have gone up slightly. Consider the Smith's—a family who likes to buy and eat lots of corn. Their money income has remained unchanged (i.e., the Smith's take home pay of $250 per week stays the same), but the lower price has increased their purchasing power, i.e., their real income. Lower corn prices mean that the Smith family can buy more of all goods, including corn, with their $250 weekly salary. It's as if the Smiths were given a small income raise when they walked into the grocery store and saw that corn was marked down from 50¢ a pound to 12¢. Their greater real income probably means that they will purchase more of the other items they like

Figure 3-1

too, such as canned tuna; but for now we are just interested in the fact that they bought more corn. We will call this the *income effect*.

The second reason for buying more when the price goes down is that we gain more total satisfaction if we buy a quantity of a low-priced good over a high-priced substitute. For example, tuna and hamburger are substitute goods: they both provide protein for family meals. If last week they were the same price but this week tuna is much cheaper, we gain in total satisfaction if we substitute the cheaper tuna for the higher-priced hamburger. This is called the *substitution effect*.

Both effects—the income effect and the substitution effect—contribute to an economic law; i.e., as you lower price, quantity demanded increases. Sometimes economists refer to this law as the *law of downward-sloping demand* because the demand curve does indeed slope downward, demonstrating the inverse relationship between price and quantity.

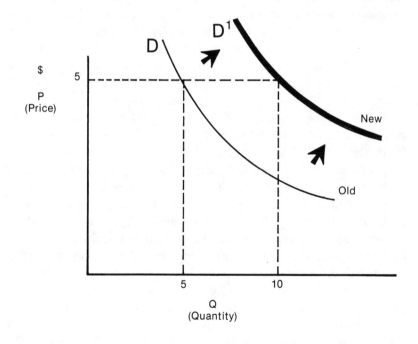

Figure 3-2

Shifting Demand

Let's now look at the demand curve from the eyes of a business-person. We learned that the curve itself is a useful tool that shows at a glance how much will be sold at differing prices. But businesses would like to go one step further. They would like to see the demand curve for their product shift to the right, which means that even *more* of a product can be sold at the *same* price. Look, for example, at Figure 3–2 and note that for any given price the new expanded demand curve shows greater quantities demanded.

Surely this is good for businesses—more goods sold at a given price. The question now arrises: "what causes the demand curve to shift?" It is not a change in price because when the price of a good changes we simply move up or down along a stationary demand curve. (See Figure 3–1.)

But what about advertising? Yes. It is commonly acknowledged that the purpose of advertising is to shift the demand curve to the right and to expand the market by increasing the number of customers for your product. Indeed, anything that brings about a broader base of potential customers will shift the curve. For example, when the United States recognized the People's Republic of China and trade between the two countries was legalized, a new market for U.S. products, ranging from aspirin to computers, suddenly opened.

What else might shift the demand curve? Let's return to our example of canned corn. Suppose that canned peas are a substitute for canned corn. What would happen if the price of corn remained constant at 50¢ per can, but the price of *peas* suddenly went up from 50¢ to $2 per can? The demand for *corn* would increase! On the other hand, if green beans (another substitute for corn) went down in price from 50¢ to 25¢, the demand for corn would decrease. The businessperson, therefore, will be watching very carefully for what happens to the price of substitute goods because this can greatly influence the demand for his or her product. In summary then, the higher the price of a substitute good, the greater the shift in demand for the product that remains low in price.

If the two products are *complementary*, however, it can work the other way around. Gasoline and cars are complementary. The demand for cars thus tends to go down (i.e., shift to the left) if the price of gasoline goes up. Businesses, therefore, must keep a wary eye on what is happening to the prices of those goods that "go with" their products.

Changes in *tastes* and *fashion* also cause demand curves to move forward or backward. Also, a *new use for an old product* will shift the demand to the right. A leftward shift will usually occur when our *incomes* go down; when incomes increase, demand shifts forward. There can be exceptions, however. A poor family, for example, whose diet consists mainly of potatoes, may experience an increase in income and *reduce* its demand for potatoes. Under these conditions, potatoes are considered an *inferior good*. Most goods, however, are what we call *normal goods*, and an increase in income brings about an increase in demand.

In a free and decentralized market, a demand curve is never stationary for very long; it gets battered around like a ship in a stormy sea. An environment of rapidly changing incomes, tastes, and prices of substitute or related goods makes it all but impossible to accurately predict the curve's behavior. In the more controlled markets of oligopolistic industries, the power of advertising causes demand curves to be more manageable and predictable than they would be in a pure-market situation.

The Supply Curve

Let's now turn our attention to the *supply curve*. A supply curve shows how much suppliers would like to provide at different prices. For example, you might ask Farmer Brown, "How much would you want to supply to the market if the price of corn were $5 a bushel?" Perhaps he would reply, "At $5 a bushel, I'd supply 35 bushels." Next you might ask him what he would produce at $4 per bushel, and so on. Let's say he gives you the following information:

P($)	$5	$4	$3	$2	$1
Q(bu)	35	30	20	12	0

Based on this information, the supply curve can be graphed as shown in Figure 3-3.

Farmer Brown's supply curve is therefore *upward sloping*. This means the higher the price, the more he wants to supply, and the lower the price, the less he's willing to supply. In fact, at the price of $1 per bushel, he does not want to supply any corn at all! Other

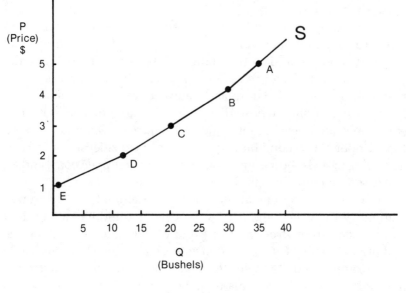

Figure 3-3

farmers will probably respond in much the same way. Instead of staying on an individual level with 35 bushels for $5, we might ask our supply question to all the farmers. For example, we may find out that 35 million bushels will be supplied at $5, 30 million at $4, and so on. The curve will have the same original shape regardless of the quantities involved.

Remember how the demand curve in Figure 3–2 shifted back and forth? The supply curve can shift too, as shown in Figure 3–4. A rightward shift in the supply curve means that at a given price, a larger quantity will be supplied. This increase in supply might take place if *more suppliers* move into the market. If businesses move out of the industry, the supply curve often shifts to the left.

Perhaps the major cause for an increase in supply is *technological advancement.* Good examples include Henry Ford's introduction of the automobile assembly line and the development of new and improved hybrid corn seeds. Shifting the supply curve to the right (through technology) has often resulted in lower prices and the creation of mass-consumption markets. On a piece of scratch paper try drawing a simple market curve with fixed demand (down-

Figure 3-4

ward sloping) and fixed supply (upward sloping); now shift the supply curve to the right and see what happens to the price.

What else can cause a shift in the supply curve? If the *costs of production* (for example, labor costs) go up, the supply curve will shift backward (i.e., to the left). In addition, certain industries, such as farming, must always contend with supply changes caused by the *weather*; extremes in weather conditions can have a great impact on food commodity supply and, hence, on food prices. So it goes—the supply curve, as with demand, is buffeted about by unpredictable forces.

Market Equilibrium

Now we're ready to go one important step farther. We have enough information to combine the supply and demand curves to form a market. Carefully examine Figure 3–5, a corn market created by putting our supply and demand curves together on the same graph. We have a visual representation of what demanders will buy at different prices and of what suppliers will sell at different prices. Note that there is *only one price* where quantity supplied will be equal to quantity demanded. This is called the *equilibrium price*; according to the graph, that price will be $3 per bushel. At $3, suppliers will want to offer 20 units of corn, and demanders

Figure 3-5

will buy the same quantity. No other price will "clear the market" in a similar way.

Indeed, what will happen if the price of corn is something other than the equilibrium price? To answer this question, imagine a large warehouse: on one side we find corn suppliers and on the other we have corn demanders. In the middle is the auctioneer, who is not aware of the true equilibrium price. Just to get things started, the auctioneer shouts out in a hearty voice, "Five dollars!" Can you see what will happen? At $5 the suppliers will want to sell 35 bushels, while demanders will only buy 5 bushels. Something is wrong. The price is too high! A surplus of corn is piling up in the suppliers' corner, while the demanders sit tight. The oversupply begins to glut the warehouse. The auctioneer realizes his mistake and has no alternative but to lower the price.

Now, however, he goes to the other extreme. He yells out "Two dollars!" Now what happens? The glut quickly disappears as the quantity of low-priced corn is frantically bought up by eager demanders. After the dust settles we find many frustrated demanders wanting large amounts (30 bushels) of $2 corn, but suppliers

are unwilling to provide more than 12 bushels at that price. Again, something's wrong! The frustrated demanders start to put pressure on the auctioneer to raise the price again. After more trial and error, we finally arrive at the final price (the equilibrium price) of $3.

In our example we had an unimpeded market where the price had complete freedom to move to equilibrium. However, in the real world prices may not be so free. Suppose that the corn farmers (who are only a small fraction of the total voters) organized and formed a political lobbying group called CORN (Corn growers Organization to Raise Net Profit). They quickly obtain hundreds of thousands of dollars that they spend on dinners and other favors for legislators. In addition, they find money left over to finance the reelection of "friendly" candidates. When legislation comes up regarding a *support price* for corn (sometimes called a *price floor*), the lobby is hard at work to get a favorable vote. After considering the bill, the legislators pass it with votes to spare. CORN is able to report back to its members that from now on the government will support corn prices!

What exactly does this mean? A *support price* means that the government will guarantee the farmers a price *above* the equilibrium. In other words, the free-market forces will be inoperative while the support price is in effect. Let's look at this situation in a graph (see Figure 3–6).

In Figure 3–6, we see exactly what effect this interference will have. If the support price is $5, we will have 35 units supplied but only 5 units demanded. Clearly, the difference between these two amounts will be a *surplus* which the government will be compelled to buy up at $5 per bushel—indeed a profitable deal for CORN! Their members can produce more corn than they would have at the equilibrium output and receive a higher price for it. Their market is stabilized, and their prices are guaranteed.

Yet it's a bad deal for most everyone else. As consumers and taxpayers you and I will pay more for corn ($5) and get less (only 5 units), while we also pay more in taxes to provide government subsidies to the corn growers. In addition, we will be paying even more taxes to finance the storage of the surplus. There are many similar examples in American industry (especially in agriculture) where the taxpayers' money artificially raises prices and thus

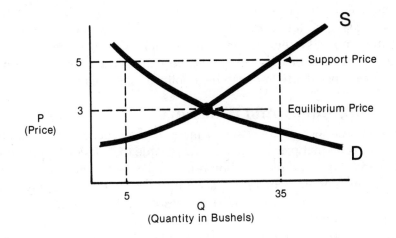

Figure 3-6

impedes free-market forces. This happens because when it comes to legislative support, special interest groups speak with a "shout," while the consumer (and taxpayer) with no special lobbyists speak in a "whisper."

Now let's reverse the situation. What if the government establishes a lower price than equilibrium? The government would in effect be saying, "You cannot legally charge more than $2 for a bushel of corn." This $2 price would be called a *price ceiling*. What happens in the market? Like our warehouse example earlier, the lower price will *generate greater quantity demanded than supplied.* The frustrated demanders want to bid up the price, yet now the government won't allow these prices to rise. A permanent *shortage* is therefore created. What then is the rationale for a price ceiling?

Sometimes the government will impose price ceilings on certain key items in an attempt to slow down inflation. But just as our example predicts, sooner or later we will begin to experience shortages. In time of war, however, shortages already exist, and the purpose of a ceiling is to prevent prices from "going through the roof." If it is a necessary item (food, gasoline, fuel oil, etc.), a price ceiling may not be enough. Often, so-called *black markets* are created in which the price is illegally bid up. (Never underestimate the power of the market!) When black markets develop, one potential solution is to allocate scarce commodities with *ration tick-ets* or *stamps*. Rationing, however, needs an expensive bureau-cratic support system, and even then black markets sometimes de-velop in ration tickets or stamps! No matter how you handle it, shortages usually turn out to be a political nightmare.

Shifting Supply And Demand

Assuming now that government price interference has been abol-ished, recall that prices *still* may change due to shifts in supply and demand. For example, as shown in Figure 3-7, after a period of wartime economic austerity, a rapid increase in the supply (S_1) can come about when new suppliers come into the market or when the industry experiences some rapid technological advance-ment. If either of these things takes place, the equilibrium price will eventually fall as a result of competition, and emergency mea-sures to handle the shortages will no longer be necessary.

On the other hand, if the supply curve (S) shifts to the left, prices will rise. This is what happens when, for example, bad weather reduces the supply of a farm commodity. If demand is sta-ble, price will increase.

Remember, too, that demand is usually not stable for very long either; recall that demand curves can move backward or forward for the following reasons:

Figure 3-7

- Changing incomes
- A change in the price of a substitute or complementary good
- A change in taste
- Advertising
- A change in the number of buyers

What will happen to the equilibrium price if there is an increase in demand? By drawing it out in Figure 3–8 we can see. You might find it interesting to examine the commodities page in the business section of your daily newspaper. See how rapidly the prices of corn, wheat, soybeans, and other commodities can change on a daily basis because of shifts in supply and demand.

Figure 3-8

Price Elasticity

Another important idea associated with demand is *price elasticity*. Let's consider a practical example relating to a person who owns a pizza restaurant. He charges $5 for a top-quality small pizza. It wasn't long ago that he was asking different people whether or not he should raise the price to $6. Of course nobody knew for sure, but some did know enough to ask him the following: "Approximately how many fewer pizzas would you sell if you raised the price by $1?" The answer to that question would help them get a feel for the pizza's price elasticity. It would be nice, for example, if he could increase his price without losing any customers. On the other hand, he might lose a great deal of his customers. Two possible demand curves for small pizzas are shown in Figure 3–9.

Although both curve A and curve B are downward sloping (remember our law of downward-sloping demand?), curve A is much flatter than B. To put it another way, curve B is much steeper than A. If A reflected the demand curve for small pizzas, would it be wise to raise the price? Probably not. Economists would say that this curve is very *elastic*; i.e., the quantity demanded is *very responsive* to a change in price. Even with a small change in price, we see quantity demanded, as shown in graph, A zooms down to less than half of what it was. Most businesses raising their price would rather have a demand curve like B, because they can raise their price without losing much quantity demanded. We call this kind of curve an *inelastic demand curve*; i.e., the quantity demanded is *not very responsive* to a price change.

What kind of products have inelastic demand curves? One example is table salt. If salt is now 30¢ a box but doubles in price, people will still demand about the same amount. However, if we double the mortgage interest rate say 7 to 14 percent, we will find a drastic reduction in the number of homes demanded. New housing would thus be an example of an elastic good.

Let's examine a few other examples. Gasoline and toy balloons are inelastic. You could raise prices a substantial percentage on both these items and in the short run not have a great reduction in

Figure 3-9

demand. Can you see a pattern that might allow you to predict elasticity? Why are some goods sensitive to a change in price while others are not? Some general principles for determining inelastic demand might include the following:

- It's a necessary good (gasoline, heating oil, prescription drugs, telephones).
- It's a small part of one's budget (toy balloons, pop, paper clips).
- There are few substitutes (insulin, light bulbs, diamond rings).

Note that salt meets all these criteria. No economic good, however, is inelastic at all prices. If we walked into the grocery store and discovered that the price of salt was not 30¢ a box but $10 a box, quantity demand would certainly be affected! In this case, you would probably learn to eat your food with less salt, and your favorite restaurant would sell you small salt packets instead of putting a salt shaker on the table.

Let's get back to the pizza restaurant. The relative elasticity of demand for the pizzas will depend mainly on how many substitutes—both direct and indirect—are available. A *direct substitute* would be a Pizza Hut restaurant down the street, whereas an *indirect substitute* might be cooking at home. If the pizza restaurant owner happens to be a monopolist and people regard eating pizzas out as a "necessity," then a price rise more than likely will benefit his business.

Is there any way that he can affect the elasticity of demand for his pizzas? He can if he can convince people that he has a truly unique, superior, and "necessary" product. Note the words, "if he can convince people"; he does not necessarily have to have a better or different product.

Advertisers for Bayer aspirin, for example, have convinced people that their product is truly different. Most druggists say that "aspirin is aspirin," but by convincing headache sufferers that Bayer is superior, the company has successfully made its demand curve *more inelastic* than it otherwise would have been. Their advertising has also resulted in a greater demand for their product; hence, they are also able to charge a higher price than most of their competitors.

Our theory has still not enabled the restaurant owner to determine whether the demand for his pizzas is elastic or inelastic. The only way to know for sure is to actually raise the price and see what happens to sales (*total revenue*). We can say with some accuracy that if you increase your price and total revenue goes up, the demand between these two prices is inelastic. If you increase price and the total revenue is reduced, the demand is elastic. Let's call this the *businessperson's definition of elasticity.*

Note that the demand in Figure 3–10A is inelastic. It should be apparent that the low-price total revenue (price times quantity) is quite small. To tell for sure, simply estimate the area of the total-revenue rectangle at the lower price (area within the thicker lines). Now compare it with the large area of total revenue at the higher price, which has been shaded in. By raising the price in the inelastic example, total revenue is increased. This is, of course, what the restaurant owner wanted when he raised his price. Note what would have happened if demand had been elastic. In diagram B we see that the increase in price reduces the quantity demanded so much that total revenue goes down.

A final point to remember: if you are a businessperson, it might be in your best interest to lower prices, particularly if your demand curve is elastic. A lower price on an elastic demand curve will generate so much more business that total revenue will go up. In addition, we often find that an expanded scale of operation will lower unit costs of production. After World War I, Henry Ford

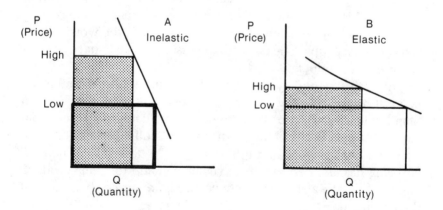

Figure 3-10

combined these two ideas (elastic demand for cars and economies of scale) and reaped a personal fortune of over a billion dollars. It pays to know about elasticity!

Let's now take a moment to review what we have learned about this subject. Elasticity is basically a measure of how much the quantity demanded responds to a change in price. An elastic curve is very responsive; an inelastic curve is not very responsive.

Also elasticity can be determined by observing what happens to total revenue (or total sales) when you change your price. If, when we raise the price, total revenue goes up, we have inelastic demand (see Figure 3–11). If total revenue goes down, we have elastic demand. Note: If you find yourself confused about what happens to total revenue when the price is changed, simply sketch an exaggerated demand curve, either very flat or very steep, and see what happens to revenue when the price goes up or down. For example, see Figure 3–11 below.

So far, so good, but we have not yet learned how to determine the precise degree of elasticity. As an example, we have two products—salt and gasoline—with inelastic demand. But which is *more* inelastic?

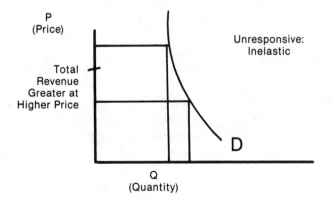

Figure 3-11

Or Let's suppose that the President of the United States determines that gasoline supplies may be threatened and it would therefore be in the national interest to reduce the nation's consumption
by 15 percent.
There are, of course, different ways to handle this situation. First,
he might ask American drivers to reduce consumption voluntarily.
If this doesn't work, he could establish a gasoline rationing system.
We know, however, that this kind of rationing invites black market counterfeiting and requires an expensive bureaucracy to make
it work. The third and probably quickest way to reduce consumption would be to raise the price to the consumer via an increase in
the gas tax.

But how much would the total price have to go up in order to
reduce the quantity demanded by 15 percent? Would a 15 percent
increase in price do the trick, or 30 percent, or perhaps even 75
percent? This question leads us to our third and most exact definition of elasticity, *the economist's definition.*

To measure the precise value of elasticity we divide the percent
change in price into the percent change in quantity demanded:

$$E_p \text{(coefficient of elasticity)} = \frac{\text{Percent change in quantity demanded}}{\text{Percent change in price}}$$

If this ratio is greater than one, it is elastic, and if the ratio is less
than one, we call it inelastic. For example, if we find out that the
gasoline price must go up by 30 percent before we get a 15 percent
reduction in gas consumption, then the exact elasticity would be:

$$\frac{15\%}{30\%} = .50$$

Since the ratio is less than 1, it's inelastic. If the President had
known beforehand that the coefficient of elasticity for gasoline
was .50, he would have known exactly how much gasoline prices
would have to increase before consumption would decrease by the
desired amount.

As another example, let's assume the demand for pizzas is very
elastic. But our friend goes ahead and raises the price by 20 percent and discovers that the quantity demanded goes down by 80

percent (he miscalculated!). Under these conditions, what would be the elasticity of demand? Using the above formula, the answer would be:

$$\frac{80\%}{20\%} = 4.0$$

The ratio is greater than 1, so the demand is elastic. In the real world, you may never know the exact elasticity. It may change over time, or it may be one value in a low price range and a totally different value in a higher price range. Still, the most successful businesspeople seem to have an uncanny instinct for elasticities and how they affect sales and profits.

Now what about you? What products do you buy? How elastic or inelastic are they to you? If the price of your favorite newspaper or magazine were raised considerably, would you still buy it? Would you buy your favorite hamburger or pizza if the cost went up 20 percent or perhaps 30 percent? These are the kinds of interesting economic questions we can all ask ourselves.

In summary, we have come a long way in understanding the workings of a market. We have discovered how supply and demand operate and how the natural forces of the market drive prices toward equilibrium. We also saw what happens when these natural forces are impeded by price supports and price ceilings. We know that the supply and demand curves shift in response to outside economic forces. Finally, we explored the mystery of price elasticity and have found out how such information can be of value to consumers, businesspeople, and government.

Thus we know quite a bit about single markets, but what about the vast interconnections between these single markets and the overall economy? What about the massive amounts of money, goods, and resources flowing in and out of millions of interrelated markets of households and businesses? How does all this fit together to form an economic system? We will soon see.

Chapter 4

BUSINESSES
AND HOUSEHOLDS

We are now ready to take a larger view of our economy. In this chapter we will enlarge our "economic vision" to include not only the single supply-demand markets discussed earlier, but also the major economic institutions of businesses and households that give life to these individual markets. Instead of using an economic "microscope" to focus on a particular market, we now need a pair of economic "binoculars" to help us see the broad outlines of our large and complex economy.

Let's begin with an analogy. The operation of our economy is something like the operation of your automobile. The performance of both depends upon two vital flows. On the one hand, gasoline (which is its primary operating "resource") flows from the gas tank through the carburetor into the cylinders where, upon combustion it produces power to run the car. On the other hand, you have the circulating flow of lubricating oil that travels around and around to various parts, reducing friction in the bearings, pistons, etc. Take away either one of these two flows and your automobile will soon stop functioning.

Economic Flows

Our economic system also depends on two vital flows. The first is *money*, which some economists consider a kind of "lubricating agent" because it makes economic exchange simpler and smoother. Money flows through resource markets (land, labor, capital) into the pocketbooks of householders, then back to the markets for goods and services, bubbling up into the business sector—a continuous circulatory stream that never ends unless the economic system breaks down.

The other flow is of *real things*—actual goods and services, land, labor, and capital. They also flow through the markets, pushed on by monetary impulses responding to supply and demand (eventually becoming used up or consumed). It's a fascinating system. Let's look at a graphical representation of this (Figure 4–1) in what is commonly called the *circular flow diagram.*

The clockwise flow is money. Starting, for example, in the upper left corner, we find dollars flowing out of businesses (expenses) into the resource markets. It is there that these dollars are translated into the demand for land, labor, and capital.

Circular Flow Diagram

Goods and Services Markets

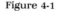

Figure 4-1

When the resources are sold to the business sector, the so called expense dollars are suddenly translated into *incomes* for the households. These dollars then flow out of the households into the markets for goods and services. We look at these same dollars and now call them *expenditures*. Demand then stimulates supply in the product markets. As payment is made for corn, auto repairs, or motorcycles, the dollars become *sales* for businesses, providing them with working capital to start another round of productive flow. The cycle thus begins all over.

It sounds like a simple, foolproof system, doesn't it? The chance of a breakdown does exist, however. There is no absolute guarantee that the money supply or the amount of total spending will be correct. For example, if the money supply is too low, the economy will slow down because of insufficient currency to make basic transactions. On the other hand, if there is too much money, we will find ourselves in an inflationary situation where there are "too many dollars chasing after too few goods." Similar problems can arise when there is also too much or too little spending.

Whose responsibility is it to regulate these flows? The responsibility lies primarily with the government sector. Along with the business and household sectors, government also plays an important role in the operation of our economic system. (We will have much more to say about this sector in Chapter 5.) For now, however, let's take a close look at the business sector. How do we define a business? How are businesses organized? How effectively do they operate in a capitalist setting?

The Business Sector

There are approximately 20 million businesses in the United States. The majority of them are small retail or service businesses and other single-proprietor operations including farming. Operating these small enterprises often means overworking Mom and Pop to keep the business going. To make things worse, they frequently end in bankruptcy. (Three out of five new businesses fail before the third year of operation!)

Let's now play a little game. Assume that you have carefully considered the odds, and you have decided to plunge into a new business. You might try to write, publish, and market your own book for example, or perhaps you would like to manufacture computer software or run a candy store. A repair service would also be a possibility. For our purposes here, though, let's assume you go into manufacturing.

The first question, of course, is "What are you going to make?" You don't wish to compete with a large oligopolistic industry because of the many economic barriers (see Chapter 2). You will obviously want a new product for which there is a need. You will probably also wish to start out with a product that can be manufactured by one or two people.

One day you read in the *Wall Street Journal* that sales of cat food have quadrupled in the last decade. You begin to think, "Yes, about half my friends have cats, and you know, their cats always want to be let in or out. Why couldn't I make an entrance/exit device to let cats enter and leave when they want. It would have to be designed so that heat is not let out, and it would have to be easy to install. . . ."

You convince yourself that you can make a go of it. You then work hard for six months on a prototype, and by the end of the year you have your cat loving friends trying out your new invention—KITTYOUT.

Now you need to think about the business end of your operation. You have several options. You may decide to set up what is called a *single proprietorship*. The proprietorship is perhaps the most simple type of business organization. It can be started up with a minimum of red tape—no charters or extensive reports needed. "A good deal," you say to yourself—until you find out some of the disadvantages. Should you want to expand your small operation, you might find that no one wants to give you a loan. You try the local banks; they smile pleasantly and say, "We're sorry." The Small Business Administration (an agency of the federal government) also lends a kindly ear but tells you that the enterprise is as yet unproven. "Please come back," they say, "when sales and earnings are more stable."

You also can face the disadvantage of *unlimited liability*, which means that if things go badly, your creditors can sue you not only for your business assets but also for your personal assets. Your child's educational fund could be liquidated as a result of a bad business decision!

Yet, you decide business is going OK for now, and your major worry at present is finding the financial capital to expand. You begin thinking of alternatives, and one comes to mind: a partner. You invite a friend (or relative) to join you and form a *partnership* in order to provide additional financial capital as well as a helping hand. There is now, however, more red tape. A partnership is a legal entity, and if your partner leaves you (or dies), you usually have to start all over. Plus, you are still faced with the problem of unlimited liability. Nevertheless, we'll assume that you and your partner are not worried much about the liability problem; sales are now excellent, and you are becoming intoxicated with visions of unlimited profits. Expansion is the only thing on your mind. You ask yourselves, "How shall we expand?"

You might, for example, take the route of *vertical expansion*. Perhaps you have been purchasing sheet-metal supplies from a local sheet-metal shop, and you now decide to buy him out. Thus, by expanding vertically you are taking over another stage of production.

Or, instead of taking over early stages of manufacturing, you might go to the other extreme of marketing the product, i.e., setting up your own shops to sell KITTYOUT. Until now you were selling them to a regional distributor, who, in turn, sold them to established retail shops. (In the larger economy, the oil industry is a good example of this. They often own or control almost all stages of production: oil wells; pipelines; refineries; and, of course, distribution through local service stations.)

Another option is *horizontal expansion*. This means doing more and more of the same operation. You might buy out the competition, or you might set up another small-scale factory in another location. Either way, your expansion activities would concentrate on the assembly stage.

Another choice open to you is expansion by *diversification* —to bring out several products. They may be related to your original product, or they may be totally different. For example, you might decide to manufacture an improved cat or dog house, or even a DOGGYOUT (using the same design and engineering principles utilized in your successful KITTYOUT).

Many large American corporations prefer to have such wide diversification that there is often little or no relationship between the products. Such a business that expands through buying up un-related businesses is called a *conglomerate*. Why would a company do this? Some economists say such behavior is sometimes a personal "power trip" or an exercise in empire building. Another answer is that conglomerates can efficiently spread their overhead this way. A small company might not have sufficient working capital to afford a business economist, a market researcher, or an advertising division, but the large parent company can afford these important marketing aids and can give assistance when needed. Diversification is also a kind of insurance policy against a sudden shift in demand away from a single-product line such as hula hoops or cigarettes.

There can, however, be a darker side to the diversification merger trend. These giant conglomerates often operate with a kind of cold detachment. They can play with the fates of factories, businesses, and employees with the calculated ruthlessness of a chess player sacrificing pawns in order to save the king. Economist Ernest Mandel captures this feeling of absentee ownership in his provocative article, "Where is America Going?":

> They retain ultimate power—the power to open or to close the plant, to shut it in one town and relaunch it 2,000 miles away, to suppress by one stroke of their pens 20,000 jobs and 50 skills acquired at the price of long human efforts.[9]

But we've gotten a little ahead of ourselves! Our KITTYOUT business is still only a partnership—not a large conglomerate. The major question facing our enterprising partnership is still, "How can we best grow?"

At this stage of development the answer to our question is probably to form a *corporation*. Among the major advantages of a corporate form of ownership are the new opportunities that are available for obtaining financial capital. A corporation, for example, can sell equity (or ownership) stock as well as float corporate bonds. In addition, obtaining a loan from established financial institutions (i.e., banks, credit unions, etc.) is often easier for corporations than for unproven single proprietorships or partnerships. *Limited liability* is another advantage of the corporate form; the debts of the corporation are "limited" by law to extend only to the corporate assets—not to the assets of the owners (as in a proprietorship or partnership).

Our partners, therefore, hire a lawyer to draw up a charter, and various friends and relatives buy into the little company. Thus, KITTYOUT, INC. (Incorporated), joins the ranks of the approximately 3 million corporations that exist in the United States. To be sure, our little company is not yet in the big time; it probably never will be. As discussed in Chapter 2, it is extremely difficult to become a major industrial company in American industry.

To get an idea of just how big some of these giant companies are, imagine a list of the 3 million or so corporations, with the larger companies up at the top and the smaller on the bottom. If we were to tally up the assets of the 200 largest corporations at the very peak of our chart, we would discover that this small group of companies (less than one tenth of 1 percent) owns *over half* of all manufacturing assets in the country! These corporations indeed dominate the mainstream of American business.

In our example of KITTYOUT we looked at the different forms of business enterprises and noted some of their advantages and disadvantages. However, we have not yet examined the inner workings of a business. How do businesses combine resources to produce goods and services? What rules, if any, do they follow for best results?

Diminishing Returns

One law of economics that businesses must be aware of when they combine resources is the *law of diminishing returns*. What exactly is this law all about? I think it's best to explain it with an illustration.

A few years ago I helped a neighbor farmer (we'll call him Chester Olson) bring in his hay. Chester has just one tractor, one hay baler, and one hay wagon; we call these his *fixed inputs*. His *variable input* is labor. He can choose to work by himself or with any number of hired hands. Chester told me that if he works by himself, he can bring in only 2 loads of hay per working day. He brings in so few loads because he has to bale the hay, pick it up off the ground, stack it on the wagon, unload it from the wagon into the barn, and then climb up into the hot, sticky mow and stack it neatly—a big job for one man!

If I help Chester, the total output per day goes from 2 to 5. My additional contribution (sometimes called *marginal physical product* [MPP]) was 3 full loads of hay above and beyond what Chester could do by himself. Because a second person (myself) increased per worker output, we can say that we were in a stage of *increasing returns*. If we add a third person (Steve), we find that total output goes up only 1 additional load to make 6 total loads. With Steve added to the production force, total output goes up but at a *diminishing rate*.

Beginning with Steve (our third person), we have reached *the point of diminishing returns*. Why did they begin with Steve? Is he lazy? No, he isn't. If Chester or I had been that third person, the same thing would have happened. The reason we find diminishing returns with Steve is that we had a fixed set of machinery to work with. If there was additional equipment, perhaps just one more hay wagon, that third person might give us a lot more loads. When we speak of diminishing returns, we therefore must assume that *all inputs except one are fixed*.

How will the knowledge of diminishing returns help Chester make decisions concerning the number of people to hire? Can we automatically assume that Chester shouldn't hire that third person? If Chester is a good businessman, he should take a careful look at how much extra money the third person's extra load of hay will bring and compare it with the cost of hiring him. To illustrate, if the value of the additional load is $50 and he has to pay Steve only $20, then it would be profitable to hire him despite diminishing returns. The general rule is to *keep hiring people as long as the value of the additional hay (the value of the MPP) is greater than the extra wages Chester must pay to get that hay*.

Chester really has it quite easy. Outside of keeping his old baler running, all he has to worry about are diminishing returns, the price of hay, and the cost of hiring an extra hand. Imagine, however, the complex decisions that must be made when we produce something as complicated as an automobile. How would you go about finding the ideal mix of resources to produce a car?

Perhaps the best way to build a car might be to simply give an engineer the following proposal: "Here is my design, tell me how to build it." A good engineer, however, should come back with more than one solution. They might say, "Here is one way to build your car that is almost completely mechanized, but here is another method that is more labor intensive (uses more human labor)." They may go on to tell you many other different ways to build approximately the same car. The bumpers might be made of plastic or steel, the engine block of cast iron or aluminum. In fact, an engineer may give you an entire book describing the different possible techniques that will meet your design specifications. How do you choose?

The answer, of course, is that for any given product, you *should choose the lowest-cost technique.* If you don't, your rivals may, and then you might find yourself out of business! It should be emphasized that in choosing the lowest-cost technique, the economy will gain in efficiency. Returning to the idea of supply and demand, we want ideally to conserve the most scarce resources and to use the most abundant ones. If a resource is scarce, its supply will be low, and if it is in demand, the resource will command a high price. In trying to minimize your production costs, you will attempt to avoid using that scarce resource. Abundant resources will command low prices in the market place. You will find yourself choosing these lower cost, more plentiful resources more and more often. It's a simple idea when you think, for example, of how much more low cost plastic is being used in the place of relatively high priced steel. Consumers, in turn, benefit by relatively lower cost products.

In summary, low cost equals economic efficiency. This constant drive to lower cost is indeed one of the most remarkable and beneficial characteristics of a capitalist economic system. Ironically, it is one of the most destructive aspects of our economic system as well. Why is this so?

Pollution

The drive to operate businesses at the lowest cost possible has also contributed to our massive pollution problem. Take, for example, Gary, Indiana. If you have ever driven past the steel factory complex in Gary, you probably had to close your window. The air is unbearably dirty. Why do the steel companies pollute the air? Do they want to increase the death rate and incidence of lung disease? Obviously not. They pollute the air and water for a simple reason: it's cheaper to pollute than not to pollute.

Of course in almost every such case there is a technology available that will reduce pollution to reasonably low levels. However, if they can get away with it, why shouldn't producers attempt to push the clean up costs onto society (i.e., make them *social costs*) instead of paying these themselves? Thus, in a strange way our capitalist system tends to reward polluters: the more pollution you can get away with, the lower your costs are, and hence the greater the profits. In a few incidents, where short-run profit making is pushed to an illogical extreme, the attitude and actions of a company are difficult to believe:

> "Profit-ability" was the 1970 slogan for Union Camp, a company whose paper-bag plant helps make the Savannah River one of the foulest sewers in the nation. The executive vice-president of the company, answering Nader's Raiders' charge that his firm was dangerously depleting groundwater supplies, replied, "I had my lawyers in Virginia research that, and they told us that we could suck the state of Virginia out through a hole in the ground, and there was nothing anyone could do about it." Union Camp's director of air and water protection noted for the benefit of The New York Times that "it probably won't hurt mankind a whole hell of a lot in the long run if the whooping crane doesn't quite make it . . ."[10]

Fortunately, most businesses don't operate with such total disregard for the environment. Nonetheless, the short-run pressures to keep costs down continue to create problems in a capitalist economy. In fact, this is what we might now call the *first tragic flaw of capitalism*; i.e., in the great efficiency drive to lower the costs of production (which is generally beneficial to consumers), we have simultaneously provided an irresistible temptation to pollute. What can be done about this problem?

In theory, the economic remedy is quite simple: force producers to pay *all* costs of production. *Neighborhood effects*, where the pollution costs are passed on to society at large, should not be allowed. Perhaps the easiest way to enforce this rule is to impose a pollution tax. The government would be saying in effect, "Until now you have behaved as if the air and water were a free resource—a free trash can that never fills up—but from now on, you will have to pay dearly for using that trash can by paying a pollution tax. In fact, we will make the tax so high that you might well consider buying your own garbage cans and collecting your pollutants yourself."

A more direct approach to the pollution problem is to state maximum levels of pollution (as the government has done with automobiles). Yet there are drawbacks to the various methods of pollution control, as you probably know if you have recently purchased a car. Prices will rise, and, in some cases, short-run economic "efficiency" will be sacrificed.

Still, why shouldn't producers, and ultimately the consumers of steel or paper (or any product from a high-pollution industry), assume the *full* costs of production—even the pollution clean-up costs? If we are truly concerned about minimizing poisons in our environment (including not only the visible pollution but also the invisible poisons—pesticides, radioactive materials, methyl mercury, etc.), then we perhaps ought to act now, not for ourselves so much as for future generations. Paying the extra price in the short run may turn out to be a good investment in the long run.

The Household Sector

The other major sector in our economy is the household. If the business sector organizes resources and supplies goods and services, what economic role does the household sector play?

Households are in a pivotal position in our economy: On the one hand, they supply resources to businesses (land, labor, capital, management), and on the other hand, they are the consumers. They are approximately 100 million household units that purchase roughly two-thirds of our total economic output each year. In what form do households receive their income? Three quarters of national income flowing to resource suppliers is in the form of wages and salaries. Corporate profits represent about 10 percent of the total, and income from interest, rents, and proprietorships combine to make up the remaining 15 percent.

Once the money's in our pocketbooks, what do we do with it? Americans spend about 80 percent of their income, and personal taxes take approximately 15 percent. The remaining amount, roughly 5 percent, is saved (Americans are not known to be great savers!). On the average households spend about 50 percent of their money on services (household operations, financial services, health, transportation, education, recreation, restaurant services, etc.), 35 percent on nondurable goods (food, clothing, gasoline, etc.), and only about 15 percent on durable goods (anything with a useful life of over a year). Columnist George Will vividly reminds us that there has been a dramatic shift away from durable goods, which, over the years, has brought about a fundamental change in American industry:

> . . . golden arches, not blast furnaces, are becoming the symbols of American enterprise. Today McDonald's has more employees than U.S. Steel. This "once great industrial giant" used to make big locomotives, big Buicks. Now it makes Big Macs.[11]

Why then are services today such a large part of the average family budget? Part of the answer is that it takes more and more repair and maintenance services (and more skilled individuals) to match the quantity and complexity of today's durable goods and components of modern housing and transportation. More important perhaps is the great increase *in the cost* of professional services (medical, dental, educational, legal, etc.). The prices of durable goods, on the other hand, have been rising relatively modestly—some product prices have even gone down in the past couple of decades (radios, TVs, computers, pocket calculators). Service costs, in turn, have increased mainly because of relatively low *productivity*. Let's look at this idea a little closer.

Productivity is how economist's measure the output gained for an hour of input; for example, a 60-word-per-minute typist is twice as productive as a 30-word-per-minute typist. Let's assume that a decade ago a factory employed 50 people and turned out 100 radios a day. By utilizing labor-saving technology, that same factory today might produce 500 radios with only 10 people, thus demonstrating a dramatic increase in productivity. But why did the factory mechanize? They were forced to do so in order to off-set the higher and higher costs of labor. In addition, they were able to mechanize without great difficulty, because it is relatively easy to adapt technology to an assembly line operation. Such mechanization thus helps to keep product prices lower than they would have been without it.

Let's now take the example of Joe the barber. Joe provides an important service to people, but he finds it very difficult to increase his productivity. There he stands with scissors, clippers, and comb, as his father did twenty-five years before him, but Joe feels he must increase his prices to match inflation and higher wages throughout the economy. Households must therefore pay proportionately more for haircuts, medical and dental care, education, government operation, and other services as long as wages continue to rise in an economic environment of relatively low productivity change.[12] Some economists feel that without substantial increases in productivity, it will be very difficult to eliminate inflation, particularly in the service industries. (There are, of course, other factors that contribute to inflation. These will be examined in detail in Chapters 8 and 9.)

Another observation can be made about households. Look around you. You will note with some interest (or perhaps some resentment) that some households receive very large incomes whereas others receive very small ones. Why are some wages high and others low? To answer this we must refer again to the economics of supply and demand.

We need both supply and demand working for us in order to reap high wages. This means that the supply of people with your particular skill must be low while the demand stays high. High salaries for doctors, for example, are not so much a matter of great skill or life saving capability as they are a result of a relatively low supply of doctors and a high demand for medical services. If we could imagine for a moment that there were millions and millions of doctors in the United States, their average wage might conceivably fall below that of a skilled automobile mechanic. In fact, back in the 1930s the American Medical Association fought hard to keep the supply of medical practitioners low, realizing that an oversupply might depress wages. The United States continues to have regional shortages of medical personnel partly because of similar high wage policies. Other types of professionals have also restricted entry into their occupation with licensing and certification requirements.[13]

In summary, if we are only looking at the financial benefit of the household, the lesson should be clear: "Seek ye an occupation with few practitioners in a market of high demand, and woe unto him who by accident or design finds himself in a market of low demand and a large supply of skilled applicants." What is your occupation or planned occupation? How will supply and demand affect the market for you?

The discussion of incomes resulting from the supply-demand situation in the resource markets leads us to our final, and perhaps most significant, observation about households in a capitalist society. Recall from Chapter 1 the basic economic question, "How does the economic system distribute the available output?" We are now able to answer that question. Output goes to those individuals and families who have sufficient incomes from the resource market *to generate demand in the goods and services markets.* If you cannot compete (for one reason or another) for a decent income, you will not have the "dollar votes" in the product markets. Supply, therefore, will be forthcoming only if there is effective demand (i.e., *purchasing power*).

A major problem arises, of course, when economic needs and demand are not even remotely in balance. For example, a family might have a critical need for nutritious food; they may even be starving. Yet if they cannot generate effective demand (because of a lack of income), no supply will be forthcoming to these individuals. An exaggerated (but real) example of this occurred during the 1930s when farmers plowed under perfectly nutritious food while people went hungry; there was insufficient income and therefore insufficient demand. It's the same situation today among our poverty groups and also in the less developed countries of the world.

On the other hand, we might find (even during a depression) a wealthy family feeding their dogs steak every day, because the income is there, the effective demand is there, and thus the economic system responds. We therefore now have a *second tragic flaw of capitalism*, i.e., its tendency to be cold and unresponsive in the absence of effective demand—no matter what the basic need may be. What is to be done about these flaws? How does our basically capitalistic system resolve these conflicts?

We deal with them primarily through government action. Government then is the third major sector in our economy. In a sense government takes over where private enterprise capitalism fails. Government is a large sector and exerts tremendous influence in economic affairs. It's time we took a closer look at its function and operation.

Chapter 5

GOVERNMENT

Why Government?

I once met a man who stated quite emphatically that society would be better off with no government whatsoever, except for police protection and national defense. "Government is basically evil," he said, "it's not only very costly, but every government action subtracts from individual freedom." He concluded that everything the government is doing now could be accomplished more efficiently by an unregulated free enterprise market system.

He was certainly right in his implication about government costs. We witnessed a virtual explosion of taxes and government activity the first three decades after World War II. For example, between 1950 and 1980, per capita income rose a hefty 600 percent (inflated value), but total per capita taxes increased over 900 percent! Looking at it slightly differently, total federal, state, and local expenditures in 1950 were 27 percent of the gross national product (GNP), while in the first half of the 1980s, total government expenditures averaged 35 percent of GNP! Thus we must again ask, "Why government? What is it doing for us?"

Of course, we have already begun to build a good case for government activity, starting with the circular flow chart in the previous chapter. To review, we might ask, "Without government who would provide for (and regulate) the money supply?" We have seen that money is essential to the operation of our complex economy, and that the amount of money in circulation must be carefully adjusted to changing economic conditions. Recall, too, our discussion of capitalism's tragic flaws. We might ask how our present private enterprise system, without government intervention, would halt pollution. How do we prevent businesses from using our air and water as "free garbage cans" in their drive to lower costs of production? Self-regulation has not worked very well, nor will it work as long as pollution-prone industries feel pressured to minimize costs and maximize profits. There seems to be only one realistic solution to this problem: the government must step in to force producers to pay the full costs of production, including pollution control.

We must also note that in many cases the pollution problem cannot be solved on the local level alone. There are two reasons for this. First, the neighborhood effects of polluted water (or air) often extends beyond the confines of a specific locality. A river does not recognize municipal or state boundaries. If some company pollutes the Mississippi River in Minneapolis, it will affect not only the residents in Moline, Illinois, but also people farther down river in St. Louis, Missouri, and New Orleans, Louisiana.

Second, national pollution laws are necessary to prevent polluters from shutting down in a state with strict controls and moving on to a more lenient state. Local governments would hesitate to stop polluters if it meant throwing people out of work.

The question then arises, "What about international pollution? Shouldn't there be worldwide laws (and provisions for enforcement) to prevent the pollution of the oceans and global air currents?" Specifically, we've already seen some severe consequences of international pollution as in the case of radiation drift from the Soviet Union's reactor accident in 1986. Also consider the continuing problem of acid rain, which frequently originates from smokestack emissions across national borders. If we apply the logic of neighborhood effects on a global scale, we must conclude that in certain cases, international laws will become necessary. The market system, on its own, simply can't do the job.

According to some observers, the question we should be asking is not so much do we need controls, but rather, will we be able to control worldwide pollution in time? Indeed, there is growing evidence that the oceans are generally becoming less habitable for marine life. Industrial pollution, garbage, and invisible poisons have been detected in almost every major ocean zone. In addition some scientists, such as Stanford biologist, Dr. Paul Ehrlich, predict the eventual extinction of a wide variety of life forms if present pollution trends continue.[14] We therefore have a growing awareness that the problem of worldwide pollution cannot be solved by the market system on its own. Government action is needed.

The other basic flaw in capitalism is its inability to meet fundamental human needs in the absence of effective demand. There are many families and individuals in our society who, for one reason or another, do not earn sufficient incomes to purchase the minimum necessities of life. Some are too old, others are disabled, many are children. There are also unskilled mothers who can't find work, and men whose skills are no longer in demand. We need to ask ourselves: "What obligations do we, as a comparatively wealthy society, have to these people?" Few would want to see them go hungry or go without shelter or minimum health care.

Consider, too, the question of social stability. In his critique of "Reaganomics" (i.e., large cuts in social programs and tax reductions for upper-income groups), historian Arthur Schlesinger, Jr., argued that our government's sensitivity to people in need has helped maintain capitalism's amazing continuity:

> Capitalism has survived because of a continuing and remarkably successful effort to humanize the industrial order, to cushion the operations of the economic system, to combine pecuniary opportunity with social cohesion. It has survived because of a long campaign mounted by liberals, to reduce the suffering—and thereby the resentment and rebelliousness—of those to whom the accidents of birth deny an equal chance.[15]

Income redistribution comes in all kinds of packages: welfare, public health, Medicare, etc. Although there is general agreement that the government should play *some* role in *income redistribution*, there is much argument over *how much* public subsidy should be available for the poor. Indeed, there are few subjects in economics that generate such heated and bitter debate. Some have suggested that income be redistributed in the form of government jobs or even a guaranteed minimum income. Should this subsidy level be at a bare survival level, or should there be enough money to provide a family with a moderate standard of living? This subject will be studied further in the next chapter.

We also need government to help maintain competition. Even the most bitter foe of government intervention can appreciate the value of some antitrust legislation. Capitalism left on its own has often produced an increasing concentration of economic power, as large and powerful firms eliminated rivals by means fair or foul. For proof, we have only to look at the pre-antitrust days of the late nineteenth century. It was an age when gigantic trusts fixed prices and monopolized manufacture and commerce with little regard for the interests of the consumer. It may seem a little ironic that we need strong *public* intervention to guarantee the survival of our *private* competitive capitalistic system, but such intervention is indeed necessary.

Without government, who would provide *public goods?* Public goods are essential to the welfare of society, yet they are either too cumbersome or too unprofitable for private industry to supply to consumers. A road is a good example. I doubt very much if you would ever consider building a highway. Even if you could afford it, why would you personally make such a large investment when a lot of other people would also be using the road—and at your expense? We wouldn't even expect General Motors or Ford to build the millions of miles of necessary roads, nor would we expect doctors to finance hospitals or campers and naturalists to totally subsidize national, state, and local parks.

What about libraries, police protection, public TV, and elementary education? These are all public goods, and if everyone is to enjoy them, we need to generate their "demand" through a system of taxation and public expenditure. Without a social commitment to financing public goods, these "necessities of a civilized society" would be available only to the relatively wealthy.

Without government who would be "the umpire" to enforce the "rules of the game"? Who would make sure that everyone plays fairly? Someone must define the legal responsibilities of business operations, someone must enforce contracts and spell out property rights. Someone must keep an eye out for misleading advertising, for foods and drugs that might impair the public health, and for unsafe products that could kill or maim thousands of consumers. We can be sure that this "someone" will probably not step forward from the ranks of private enterprise. We know that some businesses left on their own will engage in deceitful advertising or sell baby cribs in which hundreds of infants could strangle themselves or manufacture toys that are dangerous for children. In these cases and many others, we can't expect consumers to always know how to protect themselves.

But how far do we go? Where is that thin line between government as "big brother" and government as legitimate protector? We know, for example, that some people slip and fracture their skulls in their bathtubs each year. Should we require all persons to wear safety helmets when they step into the tub? Of course not. But what about requiring children and adults to wear helmets when they ride bicycles or motorcycles? Just how much regulated safety is too much? To what degree should we pursue a philosophy of individual responsibility and "let the consumer beware"? Taking this issue one step farther, when does excessive government protection tend to *destroy* consumers' initiatives to defend themselves?

We ought to also take a look at the *cost* of consumer protection. For example, would it be wise to require Detroit to build an automobile bumper to withstand a crash of fifty miles per hour? This is a good idea in theory, but how much more would this "super" bumper cost the consumer? Where do we draw the line?

Unfortunately, the study of economics does not always give us hard and fast answers to these questions. Economists, with their tools of analysis, can indeed help determine the economic costs and benefits of different actions and policies. In the end, however, such decisions are usually made by lawmakers and regulatory agencies that attempt to strike a political balance between the interests of businesses, consumers, and taxpayers.[16]

And finally, in our quest to explore government's role, we might take a moment to consider the following graph (Figure 5–1). First of all, note that the heavy line in Figure 5–1 is an approximate indicator of the age-old problem of the *business cycle,* that is the large (and sometimes not so large) swings in business activity over time. Note especially the downward trends—from the cycle's peaks to the troughs or low points. These downward movements represent times of special economic hardship which include higher than average unemployment, bankruptcies, and underutilization of resources. Indeed, we learned a hard lesson during the Great Depression of the 1930s that unregulated capitalism does not have an automatic mechanism to pull the economy out of a severe slump.

Also, during periods of extremely high economic activity, we may be confronted with a problem on the other side of the cycle;

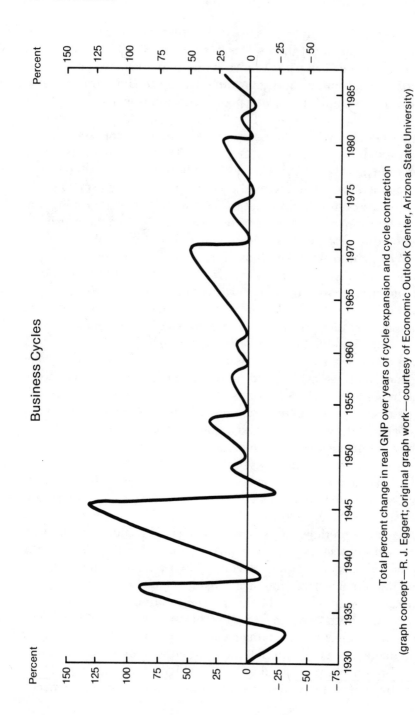

Business Cycles

Total percent change in real GNP over years of cycle expansion and cycle contraction

(graph concept—R. J. Eggert; original graph work—courtesy of Economic Outlook Center, Arizona State University)

Figure 5-1

i.e., unacceptable inflation. It is the existence of these large swings in the economy's business cycles and the accompanying problems that we will now call *the tragic flaw of pure capitalism.*

In times of slumps and high inflation, the government will therefore be pressured to take initiatives to help smooth out the severity of the cycle. Note in Figure 5–1 that though the cycle has not been eliminated, the exaggerated parts of the cycle have, since World War II, been leveled out somewhat (and their duration shortened)—primarily through government budgetary and monetary policies (more on these policies in Chapters 8 and 9).

In summary then, the business cycle forces the government to become a kind of economic manipulator who, like the white knight in the fairy tale, attempts to slay the "double-headed dragon" of depression and inflation and to generally smooth out the business cycles.

Yet as successful as governments might be in some areas, our "white knight" can also have an unpleasant side. We know that some government activity is badly planned, expensive, and (at times) downright harmful. We can cite numerous examples of overregulation and needless meddling in affairs that are none of the government's business. We have, for example, seen the effects of a top-heavy and insensitive bureaucracy.

We have also seen certain safety laws enacted that are good in theory but, when the fine print is read, turn out to be unrealistic impediments to the operation of legitimate small businesses. We have seen some bad effects from restrictive zoning and outmoded building codes as well as unnecessary harassment from inspectors, all of which can stifle innovation and initiative. We have seen government-sponsored urban-renewal programs disembowel whole neighborhoods and build public housing monsters in their place. And finally, we have seen how chilling the effects of government intelligence systems can become—an insidious world of phone taps and computer-bank retrieval systems where a sense of privacy is all but destroyed. No, not all government action is good.

But certainly some government is essential in a complex society. If government destroys some freedoms, it enhances others. Although it does so imperfectly at times, government subsidizes education for everyone, creates employment in times of recession, and enforces equal-employment rights. Government also builds clinics and public parks, supports agricultural research, and looks after the environment. It finances countless programs that truly help people who need help. Without government intervention, our complex economy would have a difficult time surviving.

The ambivalence of big government—combining both the good and bad (and often not being able to tell the difference)—sometimes creates an identity problem for this benevolent titan. Perhaps no one captured this sense of ambivalence better than did Associated Press writer Saul Pett, when he likened our federal government to:

> ". . . big, bumbling, generous, naive, inquisitive, acquisitive, intrusive, meddlesome giant . . . with a heart of gold and holes in his pockets, an incredible hulk, a '10-ton marshmallow' lumbering along an uncertain road of good intentions somewhere between capitalism and socialism, an implausible giant who fights wars, sends men to the moon, explores the ends of the universe, feeds the hungry, heals the sick, helps the helpless, a thumping complex of guilt trying mightily to make up for past sins to the satisfaction of nobody . . . a malleable vulnerable colossus pulled every which way by everybody who wants a piece of him, which is everybody."[17]

We thus can recognize the tremendous political pressures on government to intervene in economic affairs. But how does this "colossus" actually operate? For example, how is the public money spent? Exactly where are our government priorities and how does our tax system work? There are so many different taxes and thousands and thousands of areas of public expenditure (federal, state, and local), it's no wonder that the average taxpayer is bewildered. So where do we begin?

Taxes And Expenditures

Let's begin with the broad flows of government finance on the federal level. The largest single source of federal income is the *personal income tax* that many of us dread when the middle of April rolls around. In fact, almost half of all federal revenue comes from this tax. The second largest tax, contributing about one third of all federal tax receipts, is the *payroll tax* (*social security*). The *corporate income tax* is third in importance. *Excise taxes* (a tax on a specific item like cigarettes) plus *customs duties* and *estate taxes* make up the remaining part.

Where does the federal government spend our tax money? The largest single area of federal spending is domestic social expenditures—social security, health, education, and manpower training; these categories take up about half of all federal expenditures. The next largest area is for defense and defense related spending. Yet if we add the various categories that are defense-related (such as veterans benefits, interest on the public debt from American wars, international military aid, etc.) to the regular national security costs, we find that expenditures on "past wars and future defense" account for somewhere between one third and one-half of the federal budget.

On the state level, we find that on the average the *sales tax* contributes over half of the revenues; and the other half is derived from personal and corporate income taxes plus licenses, permits, and fees. The states spend over a quarter of their revenues on education with public welfare coming in a close second. Highways, health, and public safety follow third in overall importance.

The local tax scene is dramatically different. Local governments derive almost all their revenues from the *property tax*. Education takes almost half of the money; police and fire departments run a distant second. The total amount of federal, state, and local taxes spent on publicly supported education is a very large sum indeed.

It might be interesting to compare your community with mine (Menomonie, Wisconsin). At full valuation, our residents pay about $20 for every $1,000 of assessed valuation of property. In addition to my $20, the state gives our city a tax credit of approximately $4 for that amount. Of the combined amount ($24), $6 goes for city government and police and fire protection; $4 goes to the county for hospitals, roads, etc.; and the largest portion, $14, goes toward education.

Now what about *your* local taxes? How much do people in your area pay, and what are your government's spending priorities? You might be surprised at the answers!

Tax Philosophies

What are the basic differences between the taxes we pay? We generally categorize a tax as being either a *benefits-received tax* or an *ability-to-pay tax*. The philosophy of benefits received taxation is the following: "He who pays the tax ought to get the benefits from the expenditure of that tax." Perhaps the best illustration of this is the gasoline tax, specifically earmarked for highway construction and maintenance. Hunting license fees, tuition for state universities, and the airport tax (to pay for antihijacking security) are other examples. In each case the money from the tax is earmarked and funneled back into a direct service for the taxpayer. To many people the benefits received philosophy seem like the fairest possible system. But if this is true, why don't we base all our taxes on this principle?

If we used only the benefits-received principle, there would be some major problems. For example, how would we pay for national defense? Would everyone—rich and poor alike—pay the same dollar amount? That would hardly be practical. How would we finance public schools on a benefits principle? Would we only tax the families with children (and the larger the family, the greater the tax)? How then would we guarantee that everyone received an equal opportunity for a good education? We couldn't. For this reason, and others, we have the ability-to-pay tax, which does not penalize lower income groups and deprive them of the various benefits of government expenditures.

More specifically, the ability-to-pay philosophy says, "He who has more financial resources (income and wealth) should pay more tax." Many economists feel that the best example of this kind of tax is the *progressive income tax*. A progressive tax means that the greater your income, the greater percentage of tax you pay.

A greatly simplified progressive income tax became law under the Tax Reform Act of 1986. When many of the earlier loopholes and exemptions were eliminated, it made it possible to lower the maximum tax rate from 50 percent to 28 percent. And with a minimum bracket of 15 percent, Congress thus retained the progressive philosophy but greatly reduced the number of brackets compared to the earlier system.

There are also *regressive taxes*. If a purely progressive tax is a good example of ability to pay, the regressive tax is the opposite. With a regressive tax, the poor *pay a higher percentage of their income* (as taxes) than do the wealthy. A good example is a $1 park entrance fee. A dollar is obviously a larger percentage of a poor person's income than a rich person's income. Also, tuition can sometimes be considered regressive as can the property tax. For example, a home-owning retired couple may easily find themselves paying a sizable percentage of their relatively small social security income as property tax.

The sales tax might also be considered an example of a regressive tax since poor families usually pay tax on all their income (because it is probably all spent). The wealthy save or invest much of their income and thus have a sizable portion of their income that is not exposed to the sales tax. When looking at total incomes, the poor often wind up paying a higher percentage as sales tax. There are a number of states that have minimized the regressiveness of their sales tax by exempting some necessary items such as food or drugs.

Generally, most economists feel that a simplified progressive income tax is a fairer way to raise government revenue than sales or property taxes. Of course any method of taxing away spending power from the public is going to be unpopular. Taxpayer hostility can often be traced to objections to specific public expenditures. The one expenditure that is perhaps the most controversial is welfare. Let's now take a closer look at this issue and the companion problem of poverty in the United States.

Chapter 6

POVERTY

I would like to begin this chapter with a letter written to the editor of a St. Paul, Minnesota, newspaper. It has, as you will note, a somewhat bitter tone to it as the writer describes her intense resentment toward those who are receiving public assistance:

> . . . according to a newspaper item one AFDC (Aid to Families with Dependent Children) recipient said "we are people too." Yes, they "are people too," people who are unwilling to go to work to support themselves and their children as long as they are able to steal from the rest of us who have worked hard and long for many years. May I state that my husband and I and thousands of other hard working people "are people, too" who are being robbed every day of the year by these leeches who can work, but who will not work, as long as the taxpayers of the city of St. Paul are being bled for money to keep these people sitting at home listening to and watching television programs. . . . What about the rest of us who have worked all of our lives and now find ourselves "short of money" too, because we have to share with these people our hard-earned money. Where do they think we get our money?

It's certainly an honest letter. It's also a powerful letter: they "steal from the rest of us," we are "robbed by these leeches," and "the taxpayers are being bled for money."

But it's also, I believe, a misleading letter because the writer seems to be blaming all the poor for their own poverty. There are, in fact, more than 30 million men, women, and children (mostly children) who are unable to participate successfully in our competitive capitalist system. For one reason or another they simply do not earn adequate incomes to buy the basic necessities of life.

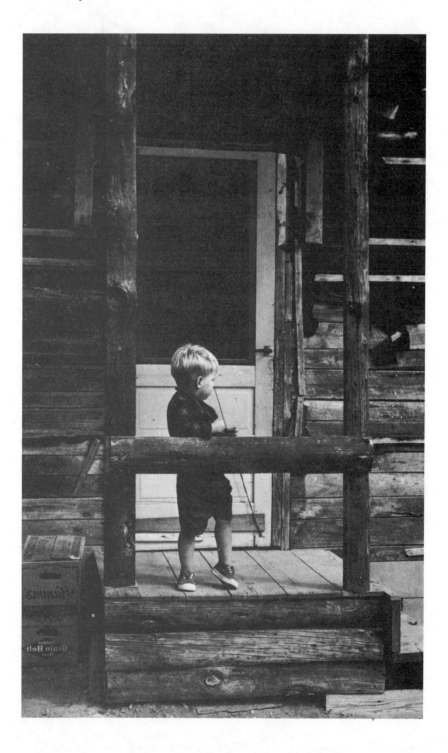

Still, research indicates that most adults want to work and will work, given the chance. For example, in half of the poverty families, at least one member of the household holds a job; in 20% of the poverty families, both parents are working.[18] Working families often remain poor because wages are too low. If, for example, a person worked full time, forty hours a week, fifty-two weeks a year, at the federal minimum wage, that person's yearly income would still fall below the income definition of poverty for an urban family of four!

The author of the opening letter was apparently not aware of some of the other statistics of our welfare programs. The federal government reports that on national average *most welfare recipients are children.* (One in five American children under six years lives in poverty!) The second largest category includes the blind, aged, and disabled. Next are the mothers of poverty children and last come the able-bodied fathers.

What about the wide-spread belief, "once on welfare, always on welfare?" This is another of the many misconceptions. Examining national averages, half of poverty families are considered "temporarily poor," being on welfare only 1 to 2 years (of the 10 years studied). One in six were "persistently poor" or receiving welfare for more than 8 years. In most cases, poverty families mix work and welfare with assistance needed particularly in times of family break-up, unemployment, or serious illness.[19]

Another commonly stated belief is the idea that "welfare's getting most of our tax money," Of federal expenditures in the mid-1980s, programs for the poor were a distant fifth in overall importance—after (1) programs for the elderly (Social Security and Medicare), (2) defense, (3) interest on the public debt, and (4) state and local aids. In many states, the assistance payment is so low that the amount does not even meet the state's own definition of poverty. Of course there are the infuriating (but exceptional) cases of welfare families that live "high off the hog": buying color TV sets, expensive new cars, and other items that many hardworking, tax-paying families feel they cannot afford. These are the cases that critics love to hear; they make the headlines and become the grist for spiteful and unverified gossip. Such criticism is generally undeserved. Most poor people don't want to apply for welfare assistance but need to in order to survive. In short, the poor need to have understanding from those who aren't doing so badly—not misconceptions based on prejudice or sentimentality, but a true understanding of the reality of poverty in the United States.

What are these realities? One of the classic books on this subject is Michael Harrington's *The Other America*. Although Harrington's statistics are dated (the book was published in 1962), his report is largely still true in the 1980s. What specifically does Harrington say?

First of all, he says the poor are *invisible*. They live off the beaten track. We do not notice the pockets of poverty in the U.S., whether the poor live in the deep southern rural areas, the inner cities, or, surprisingly, the American suburbs.[20]

He also says the poor are *politically invisible* (unlike the poor of the Great Depression), making them vulnerable to shifts in national sentiment and often powerless to initiate programs or to defend themselves within the political arena.

> . . . the poor are politically invisible . . . The people of the other America do not, by far and large, belong to unions, to fraternal organizations, or to political parties. They are without lobbies of their own; they put forward no legislative program. As a group, they are atomized. They have no face; they have no voice.[21]

Many of the poor also lack internal vitality. They may have tried to rise above their circumstances but have failed for one reason or another. Another attempt leads to another failure, until they are beaten down—until their self-respect and dignity are all but destroyed.

> And nothing to look backward to with pride,
> And nothing to look forward to with hope,
> So now and never any different.
>
> (From "The Death of the Hired Man" by Robert Frost)

Poverty Groups

The poor also belong to different subgroups that share the common problem of low income but have their own special difficulties. There are, for example, the aged. Although their poverty level has come down considerably during the 1970s (due mainly to inflation-adjusted social security and Medicare), over ten percent of this group still fall below the poverty line; especially vulnerable are widowed women over sixty-five where the percentages are higher than the national averages. A black retired woman living alone has, for example, nearly a fifty percent chance of living below the poverty line!

Other individuals are caught in what Harrington calls a *techno-logical cross fire:* technology has extended their lives (a person sixty-five years old can expect to live seventeen more years!), but it has also made their specific skills superfluous. In a culture where men and women are defined by their skill, occupation, and level of income, the people themselves become superfluous. Few authors have caught this overwhelming sense of uselessness better than French writer Simone de Beauvoir. She writes:

> The sadness of old people is not caused by any particular events or sets of circumstances: it merges with their consuming boredom, with their bitter and humiliating sense of uselessness, and with their loneliness in the midst of a world that has nothing but indifference for them.[22]

Another poverty group is the *structurally unemployed.* They are people who, even though they have skills and even though the economy may be booming, still find themselves without work. This can happen, for example, when employment opportunities disappear because of a fundamental change in technology or perhaps a major shift in consumer demand. Such structural changes in the economy often leave "pockets of poverty" that can continue for years and years. This group includes the underground coal miners in Kentucky and West Virginia and the iron ore workers in northern Michigan who watched their livelihoods dissolve as giant strip mining machines took over. It includes New England textile workers whose jobs were "exported" to low-paid Italians, Mexicans, and Taiwanese as well as autoworkers and steelworkers whose factories have been permanently closed down as the nation slowly changes from durable goods industries to services and high technology.

Other poverty groups include the migrant workers of the fruit and vegetable producing states, the marginal farmers and share-croppers of the deep South, and the millions living in the black and Spanish-speaking slums of our northeastern cities. And since *The Other America* was published, we've witnessed a surprisingly large poverty increase in *single parent households,* 90 percent of which are headed by the mother. The rise in unwed motherhood and divorce, combined with little or no financial commitment from the fathers (over half of these families, for example, receive no

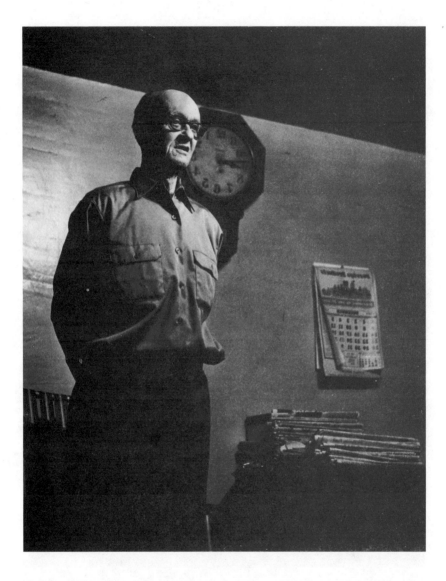

child care support), has created the most significant change in poverty statistics in the past couple decades. This is sometimes referred to as "the feminization of poverty."

And finally, there is a group, probably on the increase, that is simply called *the underclass*. The people of this group are essentially uprooted and frequently homeless. Though many are living

on the streets of large American cities, their precise numbers
are unknown as they exist outside of the regular social services
network. They include drug addicts, rural unemployed, undocu-
mented aliens, teenage runaways and nonviolent mental patients
who have been "deinstitutionalized" but given insufficient economic resources to purchase or rent shelter.[23] The American

Rick Graefe

underclass represents vivid evidence of capitalism's second tragic flaw—i.e., its inability to meet basic economic needs for its poorest and most vulnerable class of citizens.

The reality of poverty includes some individuals who were simply born with the "wrong" set of parents, with the "wrong" color

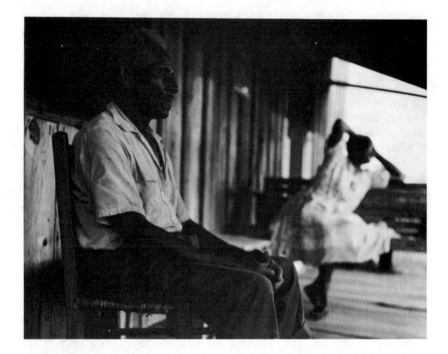

skin, or in the "wrong" part of the country—born into a kind of *vicious circle.*

Nonwhites, for example, begin with average incomes of only 60 percent that of whites. As for education, over twice as many whites finish high school as nonwhites. All the way down the list, whites enjoy clear-cut advantages in every economic category. One out of every two whites has a *white-collar* occupation, compared with one in three nonwhites. Unemployment is at least double for nonwhites in all age groups, and nonwhite unemployment among young college graduates is more than triple that of whites. When we examine the unemployment statistics for minority teenagers, we discover that between 40 and 50 percent of all nonwhite teenagers are actively searching for employment but can't find jobs! Indeed, this may be America's most profound economic tragedy— that a sizable group of young men and women are not allowed to become integrated into the mainstream of society with an entry-level job.

This vicious economic circle can be viewed as a kind of sickness—with the cure often out of the patient's control. Communities with low incomes, for example, may very likely have substandard schools, staffed either with young and inexperienced teachers (at the lowest end of the salary scale) or uninspired teachers who are not good enough to move on (even though they would like to). Lacking good models of middle-class mobility and economic success, young people receive little inspiration or encouragement and tend to drop out more frequently than middle class students. Students coming out of a low-expectation environment with few, if any, marketable skills, wind up with the economy's most menial, dead-end, and lowest-paying jobs—or no jobs at all—and thus the vicious circle begins all over again. You can start anywhere in the circle and eventually wind up in the same place.

There are other factors to consider as well, such as racial and sexual discrimination, mental and physical handicaps, poor health, crime, and defeatist attitudes. Even in the purchase of necessities such as food, transportation, or shelter, poor families find it difficult to be "efficient consumers." For example, food is often bought in smaller quantities—but more expensive per unit weight. Low-income housing is frequently not energy efficient and thus more expensive to heat in the winter. Each additional factor adds a new dimension of difficulty for those trying to break out of the circle.

Of course, there have been numerous successful breakaways, individuals who beat the system with intelligence, hard work, good luck, and frequently good connections. They are now the proud, highly skilled tradesmen, wealthy businessmen and women, bank presidents, and college professors. But like the welfare myths (the ten-children families living it up with expensive food and driving Cadillacs), these successful breakaways are the exceptions, the statistical abberations. The truth is that the vicious circle of poverty is just that—and to make headway against the odds one usually needs help.

Government Assistance

But what kind of help? Henry Thoreau once said, "If I knew for a certainty that a man was coming to my house with the conscious design of doing me good, I should run for my life—for fear that I should get some of his good done to me." Most poor people would probably agree with Thoreau's distaste for the "do-gooder," meddlesome approach. The poor often resent the battalions of government researchers and even the well intentioned volunteer workers who often irritate more than they help. This is not to say that certain government and private programs have not done some good.

We have to keep in mind, though, that poverty is basically an economic problem; its solution, therefore, must also be economic.

In short, the poor need one of two things:

a. Help in becoming economically productive

or

b. To have access to subsidized incomes

When we can guarantee everyone access to educational/training programs (plus commensurate job opportunities) *or* a guaranteed minimum income, we will have come a long way toward removing capitalism's basic flaw of "need vs. demand." But how far have we moved in this direction?

First, the question of productivity and education. Although everyone has the legal right to a free public education, we noted before that for many poor people, their early schooling is more often than not substandard—and, in many cases, even a functional literacy is not guaranteed at the conclusion of twelve years. Schools and facilities in poor districts simply must be upgraded, particularly in the basic skills areas. Fortunately many states, prodded by alarming reports and growing public concern, are making headway in this area.

Yet to be productive in a modern, changing economy, it is also desirable, even necessary, to go beyond high school. Research shows that those who continue their education do become more economically productive and thus earn substantially more than their high school graduate counterparts.

Some observers (including MIT economist Lester Thurow) have noted that, in the mid-1980s, those who attend college receive approximately $12,000 of direct or indirect public subsidy and ask why the non-college bound cannot have access to a similar subsidy. For those individuals, Thurow suggests offering "skill vouchers" worth an equivilant amount of subsidy, which in turn could

be used for vocational training.[24] This proposal, along with a high-growth, job creating economy (see Chapter 8), might indeed make a difference in upgrading living standards for people who are currently nonproductive.

Other individuals or families will, either intermittently or, in some cases, permanently, need subsidized incomes. What then are our current programs in this area and, equally important, how effective are they? Let's take a look.

Currently our government helps in two ways: *transfer payments* and *goods and services*. Specific programs direct transfer payments to certain qualified families. These programs are aimed at the elderly, blind, and disabled (Supplemental Security Income program) and to children and their mothers (Aid to Families With Dependent Children *AFDC*). Social Security, Unemployment Compensation, and Veterans' Benefits are also considered transfer payments, although they are paid to people in all income groups and not just the poor.

The second form of help our government gives is goods and services in lieu of cash. A prime example of this is the Food Stamp program. Another example is Medical Assistance or Medicaid, where the family is provided with medical care, and the bill is paid by the government. Others are public housing and rent supplement programs and energy assistance. In larger cities, there are also free medical clinics. Whether these types of service programs should be "cashed out," with the government supplying money directly to the family instead of the free services or stamps is a subject of debate. If this were done, the family could then use the cash to compete for food, housing, and medical care in the free market.

To return to transfer payments, let's take an in-depth look at one of our largest income subsidy programs—welfare—and focus in mainly on the AFDC program. We already noted the intense resentment directed toward the beneficiaries of welfare and examined some of the myths surrounding it, discovering that many of our opinions are simply not supported by fact. However, we have yet to analyze this program from the standpoint of its economic effectiveness. Is welfare good or bad? Does it help or hinder the poor? Evaluating the program as a whole, most economists feel that the present day welfare system is less than a complete success. Some feel it is poorly designed, inefficient, and expensive, often doing more harm than good in solving the overall problem of poverty. Let's look at some of the problems.

First, welfare does not always satisfy the basic economic needs of the people. Remember that in many states, the amount of welfare paid does not even meet the state's own definition of poverty. The states come up with a figure that reflects a poverty level of living, then pay the welfare family anywhere from 50 to 100 percent of that amount.

Next, the welfare system (like many bureaucracies) is often inefficient. Study the welfare procedures in your city or county or visit your local office and talk to the employees. You will soon realize that great sums of money and manpower are spent on red tape, paperwork, "means tests," questionnaires, evaluations, and investigations. A great deal of energy, money, and manpower are thus consumed by this bureaucratic machine, and as a result valuable resources are not available to the poor themselves.

Welfare can also be dehumanizing. Unsympathetic administrators can be suspicious, demeaning, and condescending to new applicants. Those already on welfare are subjected to inquiries and potential surveillance of their lives. Welfare agencies often reflect the prevailing attitude that to receive public assistance is shameful ("they have only themselves to blame"), thus, many of the poor are too proud to ask for financial help even if they need it.

Finally, our present welfare system has the unintended effect of encouraging the breakup of families. In many states, for example, a woman with children is refused aid if her able-bodied husband is still a part of the family (even though he may be unemployed). Financial pressures frequently translate into personal tensions and animosities that often end up in separation or divorce.

Indeed, one wonders why we have retained such a destructive and inefficient income-subsidy system for so long. We tolerate it partly because welfare does have its advantages. Welfare does allow children to stay with their mothers, and it does add something to the meager incomes of the aged and disabled. In addition, it has paid for health services and nursing care where they were critically needed. Furthermore, billion-dollar bureaucracies, no matter how inefficient or potentially destructive, have an uncanny knack for survival within the existing political system. Yet there must surely be a better way to deliver financial assistance to the millions of poor Americans without the drawbacks we have out-lined here. Some economists feel that, in fact, there is a superior method; it's called the *negative income tax*.

The idea for negative income tax originated with Milton Fried-man, a conservative economist and an influential maverick of the economics profession. Friedman has long advocated policies that adhere to a fundamental criterion: the enhancement of personal economic freedom and choice. He generally believes that a decen-tralized market system will best meet this objective, although it won't necessarily alleviate poverty. Friedman's alternative for our present welfare system, the negative income tax, was first outlined in his book *Capitalism and Freedom*, and since the early sixties it has gained wide respect.

To understand Friedman's idea, let's look at the income situa-tion of three different families—Jones, Smith, and Baker. We will assume that Smith has the largest income of $14,000. Next comes Jones with $12,000 and finally Baker with $9,000.

Smith	Jones	Baker
$14,000	$12,000	$9,000

What amount of federal income tax will each of these three families pay? Let's review the procedure for determining income tax with the Smith family.

Smith will not pay tax on his entire income of $14,000 because everyone is allowed to subtract certain exemptions and deductions from the gross income. Let's say that each dependent (including the taxpayer) is worth $2,000. Thus for a family of four, the total exemptions (what can be subtracted from the gross income) will be $8,000 ($2,000 × 4). Taxpayers are also allowed specific deduc-tions. Although middle and upper income families often itemize, there is also a standard deduction that is usually taken by lower-income families.

To return to the Smith family, we now know that Smith has $8,000 in exemptions. If we assume he has $4,000 in his standard deductions, the combined total will be:

Exemptions	$ 8,000
Deductions	4,000
Total	$ 12,000

Thus, instead of paying tax on his full $14,000 income, Smith is allowed to subtract exemptions and deductions worth $12,000. His taxable income will therefore only be $2,000. As the lowest tax rate is 15 percent, Smith will pay a net tax of $300 (15% of $2,000).

For simplicity's sake, let's assume that each family in our example has the same dollar value of deductions: Jones and Baker are also allowed $4,000. It should be obvious that if Jones has four exemptions (worth $8,000) and $4,000 in deductions, he will not have to pay any tax at all on his $12,000 income ($12,000 − $12,000 = $0). Baker's income of $9,000 is the lowest of the three. Baker also has exemptions and deductions worth $12,000 and thus will not have to pay any tax either.

The question of equity now arises. There is a large difference between Jones's and Baker's incomes; why does the government treat them the same? Baker has $3,000 of *unused exemptions and deductions* for which he is getting no financial recognition. If we were to institute the negative income tax, Baker would receive some kind of financial credit for his unused exemptions and deductions. The government should therefore give Baker a negative tax (i.e., a *tax rebate*) amounting to some percentage of the $3,000. Friedman suggested rebating 50 percent of any unused exemptions and deductions. Thus the Baker family would receive a check from the government for $1,500 (50 percent of $3,000). This supplementary income added to his regular income gives Baker $10,500 to spend.

Now let's look at Baker's situation if he were to lose his job. What would be the subsidy if there were no income at all? If exemptions and deductions are worth $12,000, the family would get 50 percent of that amount, or $6,000. This figure represents an *income floor*: Every family of four in the United States, even if the earned income was zero, would receive at least this amount. Negative income tax is, in essence, a guaranteed-income plan.

What about incentives? Let's suppose that after Baker lost his job he was offered part-time janitorial work at $3,000 a year. Is it to his financial benefit to take the job? With his $3,000 income he would subtract the same $12,000 in exemptions and deductions and wind up with a subsidy of $4,500 ($3,000 − $12,000 = − $9,000; 50 percent of $9,000 is $4,500). His total income would be $4,500 plus his earned $3,000, or $7,500. Yes, he is better off with the job.

You might argue that a 50 percent rate (i.e., keeping only 50¢ of each earned dollar) is not enough incentive to go to work. But there is nothing in the basic idea that says the percentage must be 50 percent. The percentage could be determined so that you would keep 90 percent (or 100 percent) of the first $5,000 or $6,000 earned. After this "grace period" the percentage might go back to 50 percent. At any rate, the percentage rates, exemptions, and deduction levels could be experimentally worked out to give enough supplementary income for a respectable standard of living and still not destroy work incentives.

We can now begin to see some of the major advantages of this program. In Friedman's words:

> It is directed specifically at the problem of poverty. It gives help in the form most useful to the individual, namely cash. It is general and could be substituted for the host of special measures now in effect.

Let's review the specific advantages. In comparison with the present-day welfare system, the negative income tax would do the following:

- It would cover all in need.
- It could theoretically be adjusted to guarantee a basic standard of living for every family.
- It would help eliminate the humiliating and dehumanizing aspects of the present system. Income supplements would be an informal matter like receiving a tax refund or social security check. Low-income families, as with everyone else, would be trusted to fill out their federal tax forms honestly.
- It would be a relatively simple system. The bureaucratic paperwork, questionnaires, forms, means tests, etc., would be replaced by an uncomplicated income tax statement.
- Social and rehabilitation workers' talents could now be directed toward helping families solve specific problems (jobs, housing, transportation, upgrading nutrition, etc.) instead of wasting their abilities and skills on the red tape involved in money transfer.
- There would be no extra financial advantage that would force a family to break up.
- It could be designed so that it did not discourage work.

There are some disadvantages as well. The negative income tax program would, in the short run, be more expensive than the present system. More people would be covered, and minimal-income levels would probably be higher. Where the money would come from is another matter to consider. In the case of unmarried or divorced female-headed households, public opinion is strong for even greater efforts to collect child support payments from absentee fathers. "Workfare," in which able-bodied recepients must accept public-service or private employment is another possibility to help pay for the programs. Eventually we may even be able to reduce our vast military budget. Friedman does feel, however, that in the long run, the positive work incentive effect (if jobs are available) and eliminating all other subsidy programs (welfare, food stamps, veterans' pensions, and perhaps even social security) would make the cost of negative income tax lower than that of all of our existing supplemental income programs combined.

Yet however we pay for it, we must first decide that we really do *want* to help the poor. We do have the resources, but we seem to lack the public will. A while back I received an advertisement in the mail called "Shop the Other America." In it was a statement that strongly supported the need for a change in our country's attitude:

> Before we can decide how to accomplish the goal of eliminating poverty, or whether we can afford to do the job, we must first decide that we want to do it—that we will no longer expect children to fill hungry bellies with Kool-Aid and candy, to be the prey of rats, to be weakened with tuberculosis, to grow up amid filth and organized vice, to be taught in deteriorating classrooms by teachers who have lost hope, and that we will no longer allow old people to huddle in lonely, heatless rooms, living on pennies, unable to afford needed medicines and services.

We began this chapter with a strong statement from a woman writing to a St. Paul newspaper and ended with another statement that is equally strong in emotion but light years away in ideology and purpose. Reconciling these two honest, but opposite views is the unfinished business of every American.

Chapter 7

MACROECONOMICS

In Chapters 4 and 5 we moved away from the "microscope" approach (supply and demand) and went on to examine the major economic sectors of businesses, households, and government. Now we are ready to take an even broader point of view. This chapter is an introduction to large (macro) economic concepts; it will be as if we were looking at the broad outlines of our economy from some point in outer space using an "economic telescope," allowing us to view the whole picture at once. Economists call this panoramic view of the economy *macroeconomics*.

You probably know quite a bit about macroeconomics already; in fact, you undoubtedly have read about it in the papers, hear about it on the news each evening, and listen to arguments about it every election year. Macroeconomics is the *study of inflation, unemployment, recession, the gross national product (GNP), economic growth, and other broad concepts of an economic system.*

Who uses macroeconomic concepts? Our economic soothsayers use them when they attempt to divine the future. Forecasters ponder charts and tables like veteran handicappers at the race tracks. They pore over income trends, savings and interest rates, consumer attitudes, housing starts, auto sales, birth rates, and other economic indicators, and then they ask such questions as, "Will we have recession or inflation next year (or both)?"; "Will interest rates go up or down?"; "What will happen to productivity?"

Then there are the popular oracles (and sometimes charlatans) of the various investment markets—stocks and bonds, commodities, and gold and silver—who use macroeconomic ideas to help them predict the ups and downs of their respective markets. A fraction of a percent change here can add or subtract thousands of dollars from a client's account.

There are also the economic philosophers who ask some of the larger human questions: "Where is mankind now and where are we going?" "What is the impact of materialism and technology on society today, ten years from now, or even a hundred years from now?" "Futurists" also utilize macroeconomic ideas and indicators.

Finally, our public officials are interested in macroeconomics. They have immediate, urgent concerns. They are like harried physicians constantly checking the pulse of the economy, anxious to learn of strength or weakness, of growth or stagnation. These are the men and women who have directly or indirectly accepted the responsibility for maintaining the economic health of the country. They include not only the President of the United States and his staff but also Congress and the decision makers in the Federal Reserve banking system.

Their economic power stems from controlling the federal budget, the money supply, and interest rates in response to changing economic conditions. A good understanding of macroeconomics is their best tool for intelligent planning and decision making.

Wealth And Gross National Product

Perhaps the best place to start our exploration of this vast area of economic theory and reality is with the idea of wealth—a yardstick by which many countries judge each other. Indeed, the United States is the envy of the world because of its tremendous man-made and natural wealth. If we were to add up the value of all our buildings and structures, our equipment and inventories, our land and other natural resources, we would be worth something over 20 trillion dollars (a trillion equals a thousand billion). This figure, however, does not tell us very much about our *current* economic health. Why? There are two reasons.

First, wealth must be utilized before it can contribute to present-day living standards. Black Africa, for example, has tremendous natural wealth, but this wealth has generally not been put to use, and, consequently, their people generally remain economically poor.

The second reason is that the value of a nation's resources in the form of wealth does not necessarily tell us anything about current production. Without a continuous flow of new goods and services, a nation will eventually consume its available wealth—like a retired couple who use up their savings and are eventually forced to sell their belongings to purchase food. Our economy, like a growing family, must have a continuous flow of income and real output if it is to maintain present living standards.

What we are looking for is a concept that goes beyond wealth, a concept that will tell us something of the total output that our land, machines, and labor produce year after year. This concept is the *gross national product (GNP)*. Economists define GNP as a measure of the final value of all goods and services produced in a year's time. Like the amount of wealth, GNP is an enormous figure— almost too large to comprehend. By the mid-1980s, for example, total GNP was approximately 4 trillion dollars per year!

We should pause a moment to consider the difficulties in computing a precise value of GNP. Of course, much of our total output can easily be traced by simply adding up total incomes (as shown on our tax returns, for example). There are, however, many goods and services that do not see the "light of day" and are never officially recorded. An unrecorded "cash" transaction (designed to bypass the Internal Revenue Service) is one example.

Probably a much larger category of unrecorded production takes place (perfectly legally) under the heading of *nonmarket transactions*. We are all a part of this "underground" market in one way or another. For example, each time we do something for ourselves that we *could have paid someone else to do*, our economic activity goes unrecorded in the official GNP statistics. Joe Smith, for example, tunes his car every six months, but Joe, of course, doesn't pay himself (and record it on his income tax). Yet if a garage had done the same work, the labor bill might have been around $50. The garage, in turn, would have reported that amount to the government as "services performed," and Joe's tune-up would have become part of our GNP.

Obviously, these do-it-yourself projects, from growing your own food to remodeling your basement, cannot be accurately accounted for in our national income statistics. The nonmarket transaction problem is considerably amplified when we note the billions of dollars of unpaid household services that are performed mainly by women. Then add to this the billions of dollars of unpaid volunteer services. Although our government does attempt to estimate the value of some of these unrecorded transactions, it is impossible to be precise.[25]

Another problem associated with GNP is our strong belief in the dictum that "happiness is a rising GNP." We often assume that when GNP is rising we are all automatically better off. Many economists, however, are now beginning to voice some important concerns about this philosophy.

For example, before we can say we are better off when GNP goes up, we first might look at what is happening to the *population* during the same period of time. If output rises by 1 percent and population goes up 3 percent, the average family will suffer a *decline* of 2 percent in their standard of living. It's a simple principle that is often ignored, especially in the less-developed countries where population growth frequently outstrips the rise in GNP.

Another point to consider is the *distribution* of the GNP pie. A rising GNP, for example, may be translated into 25 percent more housing, but if the extra houses are second homes for wealthy families, then we can hardly say that the average citizen is benefiting. Brazil perhaps is a good example of this. This South American country has certainly been a "growth economy," but the fruits of its rising GNP have been mainly concentrated in the modern sector. The majority of poor Brazilians who live in the nonindustrial economy benefit very little, if at all. Our generalization, "happiness is a rising GNP," in this case turns out to be a cruel mockery to the masses who watch income differentials widen as the years go by.

We should also consider the question of *quality*. Does the quality of our GNP change over time? Indeed, it does. Many people would argue that the quality of our merchandise and services has declined over the years. They point to shoddy workmanship, inferior materials, and "planned obsolescence" as proof of deteriorating quality. There may be some truth to this. Industry might reply, however, that the quality of some products has actually improved. Radios and televisions, for example, are cheaper and more reliable now than they were twenty years ago; radial tires are not only safer but will outlast the tire of yesteryear; and the computer of today is much better, much faster, and generally cheaper than a decade ago.

What is your own opinion about the quality of products and services? On balance, has it gone up or down? Either way, product quality is an important factor to consider when comparing GNP statistics from year to year.

Instead of looking at individual products, we might also examine the general *composition* of the overall GNP. It has been said, for example, that if we all came down with cancer, it would boost the GNP. Hospital revenues and the incomes of doctors, nurses, radiologists, and drug companies would go up—at least temporarily. Yet clearly no one could say that we were "better off."

There are thus economic "bads" as well as "goods." Many economists are beginning to look at GNP growth to try and analyze which expenditures are truly beneficial and which are not. For example, it is generally agreed that health-care costs associated with air and water pollution do not add to our net economic well being, nor do, for example, excessive military expenditures.

British economist Leopold Kohr has identified a whole range of products (and services) that he labels *density commodities.* These goods are purchased by consumers, government agencies, and businesses simply to *offset the impact of living in a high density environment* and among large scale social institutions (schools, businesses, cities, etc.).[26] Density expenditures include the cost of traffic accidents, many legal services, commuting expenses, escapist media, illegal opiates, prescribed relaxants and stimulants, and the ever more powerful headache remedies ("Life got tougher, so we got stronger," says an Excedrin advertisement). Add to this list those expenditures associated with crime (squad cars, prisons, protective services, exotic burglar alarms and foolproof locks, personalized handguns, mace, etc.), and you begin to get an idea of how much of our GNP is devoted to these goods. We are forced to purchase density goods, says Dr. Kohr, not because they offer us a net improvement in our standard of living, but because we have evolved a society where such goods are a necessity to offset the negative side effects of modern urban life. Again, the billions and billions of dollars spent on these types of goods may not add much to the net welfare of the population, yet they are all counted as part of our official GNP statistics.

Another related idea is the question of *balance and priorities.* Are we spending too little on civilian public goods such as parks, education, libraries, mass transit, rehabilitation of the cities, and too much on private goods? Economist John Kenneth Galbraith suggests this in his book, *The Affluent Society*:

> The family which takes its mauve and cerise, air conditioned, power-steered, and power-braked automobile out for a tour passes through cities that are badly paved, made hideous by litter, blighted buildings, billboards, and posts for wires that should long since have been put underground . . . They picnic on exquisitely packaged food from a portable icebox by a polluted stream and go on to spend the night at a park which is a menace to public health and morals. Just before dozing off, amid the stench of decaying refuse, they may reflect vaguely on the curious unevenness of their blessings. Is this, indeed, the American genius?
>
> . . . the penultimate Western man stalled in the ultimate traffic jam slowly succumbing to carbon monoxide, will not be cheered to hear from the last survivor that the gross national product went up by a record amount.

Since Galbraith wrote those lines in the 1950s, the arguments over GNP and the quality of life have taken a quantum leap. The battle lines are being drawn. A large group of intelligent and serious individuals contend that economic growth should be halted to preserve the environment and conserve the remaining nonrenewable resources. Zero GNP growth is their goal. In this group would be Herman E. Daly and Paul Ehrlich and the Zero Population Growth (ZPG) movement. Perhaps the extreme side of this position is that of Professor Ezra Mishan of the London School of Economics. Consider, for example, his comment:

> You could very well have stopped growing after the First World War. There was enough technology to make life quite pleasant. Cities weren't overgrown. People weren't too avaricious. You hadn't really ruined the environment as you have now.[27]

Most economists continue to be defenders of growth, agreeing with Adam Smith's historic contention that "the progressive state is in reality the cheerful and the hearty state to all orders of society. The stationary is dull, the declining, melancholy."

One might also pause to consider Irving Kristol's argument that growth is, in fact, a *necessary precondition* to a modern democracy where "the expectations of tomorrow's bigger pie, from which everyone will receive a larger slice . . . prevents people from fighting to the bitter end over the division of today's pie."[28] Defenders of growth also point out that very few families can say that they are satisfied with their current economic status. In addition, they remind us that we still have many low income people in the United States who are likely to be permanently poor in a zero-growth economy. Finally, the pro-growth people point out that it is much easier to deal with pollution in a growing economy. Cleaning up the environment will be expensive, and the additional resources must come from somewhere.

These defenders of growth are greatly disturbed that an increasing number of people want to go back to the "good old days"—those days that the pro-growth people believe were not so good. They ask, "Why can't the environmentalists understand that technology and economic growth conquered nature for the benefit of mankind?"

Author Mel Ellis, a naturalist who has demonstrated a unique sensitivity for both economic and environmental problems, once wrote:

> Man almost literally made the cow, the fat corn kernel, the plump turkey, the beautiful rose. And if he erred in his enthusiasm and polluted his raw materials, his resources, he still made the world enormously better.[29]

I think most environmentalists do understand the benefits of technology, progress, and economic growth, but their attention is directed at different concerns. They are listening to different sounds. Essayist E. B. White once summed up this attitude with the comment, "I would feel more optimistic about a bright future for man if he spent less time proving that he can outwit Nature and more time tasting her sweetness and respecting her seniority."[30]

Their immediate concerns are not with the eradication of poverty or the benefits of high-speed air travel or the advantages of the computer over the abacus. They do not see a thousand acres of timber as so many completed homes; instead they see the grandeur of the forest and its enduring value as a generator of oxygen, a climatic stabilizer, and a habitat for wildlife, and they work for its preservation. Instead of seeing Appalachian hills as a source of strip-mined coal to heat homes, they ask, "What will be the adverse consequences of strip-mining for the land and its inhabitants?"

The D-9 bulldozer is the largest built by the Caterpillar Tractor Corporation. It weighs some forty-eight tons and is priced at $108,000. With a blade that weighs five thousand pounds, rising five feet and curved like some monstrous scimitar, it shears away not only soil and trees but a thousand other things—grapevines, briars, ferns, toadstools, wild garlic, plantain, dandelions, moss, a colony of pink lady-slippers, fragmented slate, an ancient plow point, a nest of squeaking field mice—and sends them hurtling down the slope, an avalanche of the organic and the inorganic, the living and the dead. The larger trees that stand in the path of the bulldozer—persimmons, walnuts, mulberries, oaks, and butternuts—meet the same fate. Toppled, they are crushed and buried in the tide of rubble.[31]

Along the same line, who could not empathize with novelist James Michener's saddened feelings described after he returned to the site of his boyhood stream?

This marvelous stream in which I used to fish and where as a boy I had gone swimming, this ribbon of cool water which had been a delight to generations of farmers, was now a fetid body of yellowish water with not a living thing in it. Frogs, fish, waterlilies, bullrushes and ducks' nest had all vanished . . .

The loss of my stream had occurred under my nose, as it were, and with me making no protest. When I finally saw what had happened, I was ashamed of my inattention. What in those years had I been doing that was more important than saving a stream? If we continue to abuse and destroy our resources, many of us will be asking that question thirty years from now, but by then it will be too late, and some of the precious things we have lost will not be recoverable.[32]

Environmentalists, in short, are distressed by the ugliness of overdevelopment. They are angered by worldwide pollution and by the growing lists of endangered species, and they feel that these are the unnecessary consequences of man's selfishness. They are saddened by our blindness—a blindness to the real possibility that much of what we value today may be lost forever. Of those who favor "development at any cost," the environmentalists ask, "Why can't you see what uninhibited growth is doing to those things we must preserve for future generations?" The great debate over growth is based on simple, yet profound, differences in values. It will, undoubtedly, remain one of the major public issues for years to come.

Consider one more major challenge to the notion: "happiness is a rising GNP." Imagine the following scene: George Franklin and his wife Mary were overjoyed when their joint income was increased to the $35,000 a year level; the couple had never dreamed they would make that much money. Yet by the end of the year, the Franklin family felt poorer than ever. Not only had they failed to save any money, but Mary Franklin claimed that their standard of living was worse now than it was five years ago. What went wrong?

The answer to this question should be obvious since we are all adversely affected by the same economic malady. The problem was a rise in the general price level—that is, what economists commonly call *inflation*. Not only does inflation distort and diminish your income, my income, and the Franklin's income, but inflation also distorts the GNP statistics.

A simple example can illustrate this point. Let's pretend that the U.S. economy produces only one product, wheat. We will assume a time period of three years and watch what happens to GNP when the wheat price is inflated from $1 to $5 per bushel.

Year	Output (bu of wheat)	Price/bu	GNP (Price × output)
1	3	$1	$ 3
2	5	$4	$20
3	9	$5	$45

Take a look at the GNP column. If someone gave you only the GNP figures ($3, $20, $45), would you say these figures were a good representation of output? Of course not, because they are not giving you the whole story. The GNP figures are, in fact, greatly inflated compared with the increase in actual output of wheat: GNP increased to fifteen times its original value (from $3 to $45), while output went up only three times (from 3 to 9 bushels). In short, if all you saw were these GNP statistics, you would have a very distorted picture of the economic situation. Economists have a name for this "distorted" or inflated GNP; they call it *money GNP*. Using the same idea, we can now see why George Franklin felt a little bewildered when he discovered that his money income did not seem to give him any additional purchasing power. Money income and money GNP are, by themselves, inaccurate indicators of the real economic situation.

Unfortunately, the money GNP is the figure that is commonly quoted by newspapers, public officials, writers, and teachers. The 4 trillion dollar figure mentioned earlier was, in fact, money GNP. Is there any way of getting a more accurate picture of our GNP? What we need is a realistic value for GNP in which we remove the impact of inflated prices.

To adjust for inflation, we must compare each year's output with the wheat price of a single *base year*. We could choose any of the three years for your base, then apply this base year price to all the other years. For example, let's choose year 1 as our base. We then multiply the base year price ($1/bu) times the actual output of the other two years. The result is *real GNP*, which, as you can see in the table below, gives us a much more accurate picture of each year's production than did money GNP.

Year	Output (bu)	Real GNP	
1	3	$3	
2	5	$5	Year 1 = Base Year
3	9	$9	

Of course the United States does not produce one product but millions and millions of goods and services. How do we adjust for inflation when there are so many different prices to consider? The same principle applies, i.e., we use base-year prices to compare output of all the other years. The only difference is that now we must average the price changes of many goods instead of just one. This average price level can easily be summarized in one statistic called the *price index* (or *GNP price deflator*). The price index for the base year is always equal to 100 (no matter which year we choose), and any change in price will be reflected by a percentage change in the index.

For example, if we use 1982 as the base year (price index = 100), and we find that between 1982 and 1985, prices, on the average, went up 11.7 percent, then the price index for 1985 would be 111.7. Knowing that the index was 111.7, we could then convert the output of 1985 into "1982 dollars." This would give us the real GNP for 1985.

Suppose, therefore, you hear someone reporting that our GNP in 1985 was $3,993 billion. You now know that this person is giving you the inflated figure of money GNP. So how do you calculate real GNP for 1985? You would simply divide the price index for 1985 (111.7) into the money GNP ($3,993 bil.) and then multiply your answer by 100. On a piece of scrap paper you thus make the following computation:

$$Real\ GNP(1985) = \frac{\$3993\ bil.}{111.7} \times 100 = \$3575\ bil.$$

Now you know the value of real GNP (1982 prices) for the year 1985. The $3,575 billion figure is thus somewhat less than the inflationary $3,993 billion figure that was originally quoted. Unfortunately, the distinction between real and money GNP is rarely made, and the public therefore is often misled.

We are now prepared for what might be called "The Shortest Economic History Course Ever," as we sum up fifty years of U.S. economic history—in less than a page!

Year	Money GNP ($bil)	Price Index (1982 = 100)	Real GNP ($bil)
1930	91.2	14.2	642
1935	72.8	12.5	582
1940	100.4	13.0	772
1945	213.4	15.7	1359
1950	288.3	23.9	1206
1955	405.9	27.2	1492
1960	515.3	30.9	1668
1965	705.1	33.8	2086
1970	1015.5	42.0	2418
1975	1598.4	59.3	2695
1980	2732.0	85.7	3188
1985	3993.0	111.7	3575

(1982 = Base year)
Source: BEA U.S. Department of Commerce

Do you notice any interesting trends in these figures? If you read them carefully, you will notice four major economic events in this fifty-year history.

The first significant event is the deflation (a drop in prices) and the great depression of the 1930s. It was an insecure decade for Americans with high unemployment, a severe drought, and widespread poverty.

The second period of interest is the great upsurge of real economic growth from the early 1940s to the late 1960s. In an accounting sense, this thirty-year period was a phenomenal age of American prosperity. The decade of the 1960s alone averaged nearly 4½ percent *real* growth per year! By the middle of this decade political writer Theodore White would write in his book, *The Making of the President,* 1964:

> There was no doubt that John F. Kennedy and his economists had brought about the first fundamental change in American economic policy since Franklin D. Roosevelt—and the nation glowed with a boom that was one of the world's wonders. The boom terrified Europeans, angered the underdeveloped in the world, baffled the Russians.[33]

Yet only five years later, after our long Vietnam war, the glow of economic boom and prosperity turned into a bonfire of inflation, the third major event of this period. During the 1970s overall prices in the United States rose some 94 percent—a greater percentage increase than in any other comparable period!

And finally, we come to the fourth and most recent period. If the 1970s were characterized by unprecedented inflation, we find the 1980s to be an era of *phenomenal disinflation*—that is, a rapid, even astonishing, decline in the inflation rate. It began by a tight monetary policy initiated in the fall of 1979 and was fortified by a severe recession, greater international competition in manufacturing (plus a high value of the dollar making imports less expensive), and the collapse of OPEC, the international oil cartel. Few, if any, of America's best economic forecasters foresaw the magnitude of this inflation rate reduction[34]—from the 9–10 percent range in 1979, 1980, and 1981, down to 3–4 percent by the middle of the decade! Though setting the stage for a more stable economy, the sudden drop in inflation was accompanied by additional unemployment and a large number of bankruptcies, especially in the farm, oil, and mining industries.

Thus it is unemployment and, at times, inflation, that mar much of our economic history and continue to plague us as we approach a new century. We will now examine these two extremes of economic sickness in more detail in our continuing exploration of macroeconomics.

Chapter 8

UNEMPLOYMENT AND INFLATION

What do you think would happen if everyone in the United States woke up one morning and decided that from now on they would spend only one-half the amount of money that they had been spending? A very unlikely situation, yet suppose it really happened. What would be the total economic effect of this group decision?

The effect would be very large indeed. To see the impact of this large spending cutback, let us pull out our economic microscope once again and focus in on one small retail store—Joe's Super Sport Shop of Plum City, Washington. Joe's business will, in effect, become a microcosm of what will be felt by businesses all across the country. What will happen first?

Joe will immediately begin to notice that fewer customers are coming in. Before long, he may let go one of his part-time clerks. But for Joe himself, so far, so good. He is not yet facing any major problems. As time goes on, however, he begins to notice something very disturbing: *his inventory is piling up*. As Joe walks into the back storage room, he stumbles over a large box of unsold baseball mitts that he had ordered earlier according to his usual needs. Things are a little more serious now.

Most likely, Joe will try to get rid of his excess mitts by putting them on sale. Even more important (to the economy), though, he will probably send a message to the baseball mitt distributor in Seattle to hold off on any more shipments.

The bad news is channeled up to Ajax Mitt Manufacturers, Inc., of Blackstone, Maine. Ajax, in fact, is getting the same bad news

from all its distributors around the country. At first the Ajax company cuts overtime, but they soon realize that in order to avoid a pileup of inventory, they must lay off 30 percent of their work force. The directors meet in emergency session to discuss the new plant that is scheduled for ground-breaking ceremonies next week. They decide to halt indefinitely all expansion plans.

Of course, similar actions are being taken by other industries throughout the nation. Major layoffs take place in the auto, steel, and housing industries, and orders for new plants and equipment are reduced to a fraction of last year's level. National unemployment soon rises to 25 percent.

With many people on a reduced income (or no income), spending falls to lower levels, and the downward spiral continues to drag the economy down even further. What is the result of this seemingly simple decision to curtail spending? It has brought us a devastating depression! Thus, the major cause of recession, depression, high unemployment, etc., is that *somewhere in the economy enough individuals or groups of people decide (for any number of reasons) to spend less.* These people do not necessarily have to be consumers; they can be some other major spender in our economy such as businesses or government. Economists summarize the three major categories of spending as:

- Consumption expenditure (C)
- Business investment (I)
- Government expenditures (G)

Thus we can now say that any large reduction in C, I, or G spending will set forces into motion that can lead to a recession or possibly a depression.

Returning once again to our example, let's assume we are now going through the stage called *recession.* What is a recession, and how does it differ from a depression?

Recession Versus Depression

Economists say we are in a recession when the economy experiences at least a half year of declining real GNP. By this definition, our economy has experienced eight recessions since World War II: 1949, 1954, 1958, 1960, 1970, 1974, 1980, and 1982. In terms of unemployment, the most severe of our recent recessions was in

1982 when, for a number of months, over 10 percent of the labor force was out of work. The mildest recession was in 1970, with only 5 percent unemployment.

If a recession is a bad cold, a depression is pneumonia. In effect, *a depression is a severe and prolonged recession.* The great depression of the 1930s, for example, lasted approximately a decade with unemployment rates ranging from 12 to 25 percent (1933). In no year during the decade of 1931 to 1941 did the national jobless rate drop below the 10 percent figure!

Depressions have a touch of economic insanity. During the 1930s, there were idle machines and idle men and women who *could* have been producing goods and services the nation desperately needed, but the unemployed people sat idle, and their machines rusted—and nobody knew what to do about it.

There was a comparable tragedy in the countryside as well. In one part of the nation, fruit and grain ripened and livestock fattened in our great fertile valleys, but the farmers destroyed the livestock, burned the grain, and let the ripened fruit rot while people went hungry because many had little or no income and therefore no purchasing power. Writer Caroline Bird, in her book *The Invisible Scar*, retells a number of anecdotes that illustrate some of the sadness and suffering during those years:

> Miners tried to plant vegetables, but they were often so hungry that they ate them before they were ripe. On her first trip to the mountains, Eleanor Roosevelt saw a little boy trying to hide his pet rabbit. "He thinks we are not going to eat it," his sister told her, "but we are . . ." (pages 26–27)
>
> A year after his defeat by Roosevelt, Hoover—who had repeated so many times that no one was starving—went on a fishing trip with cartoonist "Ding" Darling in the Rocky Mountains. One morning a local man came into their camp, found Hoover awake, and led him to a shack where one child lay dead and seven others were in the last stages of starvation. Hoover took the children to a hospital, made a few phone calls, and raised a fund of $3,030 for them. (page 39)

In addition, disastrous weather conditions in some parts of the country added to the general economic suffering. In the Midwest wheat and corn belt there were desperate, bankrupt farmers who choked on dust from the worst drought that anyone could remember. There seemed to be some malicious and sinister force in the air that paralyzed economic activity and turned topsy turvey the economic laws that had always worked for our benefit—a force that almost broke our spirit:

> The women studied the men's faces secretly, for the corn could go, as long as something else remained. The children stood nearby, drawing figures in the dust with bare toes, and the children sent exploring senses out to see whether men and women would break. The children peeked at the faces of the men and women, then drew careful lines in the dust with their toes. Horses came to the watering troughs and nuzzled the water to clear the surface dust. After a while the faces of the watching men lost their bemused perplexity and became hard and angry and resistant . . . Then the women knew that they were safe and that there was no break. Then they asked, What'll we do? And the man replied, I don't know . . . But it was all right . . .

(From The Grapes of Wrath by John Steinbeck)

We now know something of what that "sinister force" was. It was by a large reduction in spending in all major sectors of the economy set off by the great stock market crash of 1929.[35] This inability of pure capitalism to regulate itself—that is, its inability to avoid the ups and downs of a business cycle is, as we noted before, capitalism's *third tragic flaw*. We will soon see how this problem is dealt with in a modern economy. First, however, let's go back to the example at the beginning of the chapter.

Remember we had first decided to spend less, then quickly found ourselves in a recession, and then later dropped into a deep depression. Let's now assume that after this unhappy time people, businesses, and government decide to begin spending again. What will be the new scene at Joe's Super Sport Shop?

Joe's business immediately picks up, forcing him to rehire his part-time help. He no longer trips over surplus boxes or baseball mitts. In fact, when Margie Miller comes in to buy her autographed Lou Gehrig Little League baseball mitt, Joe discovers that he is all sold out. He quickly dials his distributor in Seattle, who at that very moment is writing purchase orders to the Ajax Mitt Co. Ajax immediately rehires laid-off workers as the plant gears up for full-capacity production. Finally, the directors of Ajax, Inc., meet and approve the ground breaking for not one but two new Midwest plants.

Happy times have returned. Things are humming along in all of the economy's major industries. Everyone appears satisfied as more and more expenditures flow through the system, buying up greater and greater amounts of goods and services. Notice too that once there is upward motion in the economy, everything tends to reinforce the trend—greater spending generates more employment, more income, and more investment spending. Each of these new spending dollars in turn generates another round of spending and enlarged incomes. The pace accelerates—perhaps too fast. At some point the total demand begins straining the available supply as resources become fully employed. The result is *the beginning of inflation as a large number of dollars "chase" after a limited supply of output.*

At first, of course, there is not much to worry about. A few prices pop up here and there as inventories are depleted; product shortages are a little more frequent than before. Yet if demand expands too fast, the existing plant capacity will soon become overloaded as we reach full utilization of our labor force and industrial capacity. Businesses will be under pressure to expand to meet the demand, yet there simply won't be enough resources! As they attempt to buy existing raw materials and to attract skilled labor, businesses find they have to pay more and more. Labor unions will be quick to take advantage of the "seller's market" for labor, and before long wages are pushed up. Businesses don't mind too much since they can usually pass their increased costs on to the consumer in the form of higher prices. Inflation that results from higher costs is often referred to as *cost-push inflation*. Higher labor costs, however, mean fatter pay-checks. This extra demand pulls prices up again (too many dollars chasing after too few goods), and we experience another round of demand-pull inflation.

These two factors (excess demand, higher costs) pull and push the economy again and again, as if bending a wire back and forth. The heated-up economy soon reaches a breaking point. This *hyperinflation* can be as devastating to an economy as a depression; both are extremes that can and must be avoided. We will look at more details of these two problems in a moment, but first, let's summarize what we have learned thus far.

The diagram in Figure 8–1 looks something like the supply and-demand graph in Chapter 3. Here, however, the up-and-down axis represents the overall price level. Any upward movement on the price scale can be directly translated into inflation. The bottom axis represents output and employment. If output is high, we know employment will also be high; if output is low, employment will be low as well. Since both values are directly related, we will simply call the bottom axis "Employment and Output." We might give our diagram the following title: "What More Spending Does to Prices, Employment, and Output."

Let's begin at point A (in the midst of the depression). Note the relatively low price level combined with a small GNP and high unemployment. As we begin to spend more, we move along the solid line to the right. Each additional dollar spent means greater employment and output *without* any inflation penalty. This remains

What More Spending Does to Prices, Employment and Output

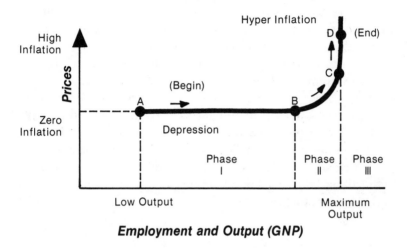

Figure 8-1

true all the way through Phase I, until we reach point B. After B any additional spending not only brings greater output but also some degree of inflation. We call this Phase II or the *trade-off* area. In other words, if we want higher levels of output and employment, we must accept a trade-off in the form of higher prices. Once we reach C, however, what happens? If we spend beyond point C, we gain nothing in output and employment (because the economy is operating at maximum output), but we completely lose out because of hyperinflation.

We might generalize and say that to operate in either Phase I or III is a great mistake since we can gain employment (without any inflation penalty) in Phase I, but Phase III represents nothing more than sustained inflation (with no employment advantage). No, the logical place to operate (if we are in control of things) is in the trade-off area. Let's magnify this section of our graph (see Figure 8–2) to see precisely how it operates.

The reality of trade-off is actually a variation of the old saying, "you can't have your cake and eat it too"; i.e., we can't have full employment and zero inflation at the same time. Trade off thus forces us to choose which objective we value most—high employment or low inflation. For example, if we operate in the Stage 1 area of trade-off, we are choosing a low-inflation, high unemployment situation. On the other hand, if we choose an area near Stage 3, we are opting for full employment with high inflation. It often boils down to a very difficult political decision. Have you ever heard the statement, "If we are ever going to solve our bad inflation problem, we may have to have a recession"? This is the sort of hard choice the trade-off dilemma forces us to make. How then do we choose? Can we tell which of these problems—inflation or unemployment—is going to give us more trouble? Economists can't say for sure since each of these problems affects us differently. Let's therefore take a closer look at the specific economic impact of both these economic maladies.

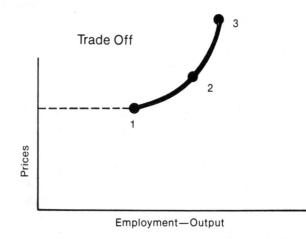

Figure 8-2

Inflation

First, consider inflation. Exactly why is inflation bad? Most people have jobs during high inflationary periods, and inflation by itself does not normally reduce output. The problem with inflation is that *it distorts the economy*; it redistributes large portions of the economic pie away from some people and places that income into the hands of others—often unfairly or free of charge.

Indeed, some groups do fairly well during inflationary times. Anyone on a *flexible income*, for example, will usually do all right. Labor unions with bargaining clout (and inflation based escalator clauses in their contracts) tend to benefit. So may large corporations. Since demand is usually high, these businesses are often able to raise their prices in response to higher labor and raw material costs. The *speculator* who purchases property, gold, etc., at bargain prices and then sits back to "let inflation do its work" also benefits from inflation. Finally, those who *borrow* large amounts of money often find themselves in good shape during this period because they will be able to pay back their loans in easy-to-come-by inflated dollars.

It shouldn't be difficult to see which groups are the hardest hit by inflation. *Fixed-income* families suffer the most, including, among others, the millions of marginal workers in low paying industries with no unions, retail clerks, hotel and restaurant workers, and others who work at or below the minimum wage.

With borrowers gaining because of inflation, lenders often lose out, as do savers who are forced to sit back and watch (with great bitterness) their saved-up purchasing power evaporate under the heat of rising prices. The so-called virtues of a nation—hard work and thriftiness—become cruel hoaxes, and the vices of speculation and excessive borrowing are rewarded. Inflation thus becomes an insidious disease that saps economic incentives, a disease that renders people unsure of the present economic reality and fearful of what the future will bring.

Unemployment

Now let's look at the other side of the trade-off dilemma—unemployment. To be unemployed means more than "just not having a job." By definition, a person is unemployed if they are actively seeking employment (by registering at employment offices, etc.) but cannot find work.

Surprisingly, not all unemployment is undesirable or harmful to the economy. Economists say there is about 4 percent *frictional unemployment*; those in this category are looking for work for the first time or are voluntarily changing jobs. They are indeed actively seeking work, but their situation is not terribly serious. In fact, without some frictional unemployment our economy would lose a measure of efficiency that is brought about by labor mobility. Since there is no way to reduce this kind of unemployment (nor would we necessarily want to), we can say that our economy is "fully employed" when we are at or near this 4 percent level. Or putting it slightly different, when 96 percent of the labor force is employed, we could say our economy is operating at "full capacity."

There are, however, other categories or types of unemployment that are more serious and often more intractable. For example, at any given time, there is a group of unemployed that economists call *discouraged workers*. They've simply given up hope of finding work. We don't know who all these discouraged unemployed are, but they include, among others, married, college educated women who would like a good job but can find nothing available where they live and lack the mobility to move to where the jobs are. There are middle-aged men and women who are fired, phased out, or laid off (indefinitely). These individuals may have worked for years, but now they find out that no one wants to hire them. There are also many Americans from minority groups who have simply given up trying to find jobs because of racial discrimination. These are just a few examples of the disappointed dropouts who exist in an economic limbo.

Then there are also the *structurally unemployed*. We already know (from Chapter 5) something about this group. They are workers whose skills have become obsolete or whose jobs disappeared when the factory or mining operation shut down. They are workers whose problems cannot be readily solved by more spending and greater economic expansion. They therefore need retraining for new skills and often need assistance to relocate to areas where jobs are available.

Finally, we come to *Keynesian unemployment*, named after British economist John M. Keynes. This kind of unemployment results from a lack of spending and the resulting business cycle downturn as described at the beginning of the chapter. It was Keynes who first devised the theory that such unemployment can be significantly reduced by instituting government programs designed to stimulate additional spending. This was indeed a revolutionary idea since few economists before Keynes had ever dreamed of manipulating an economic system.

Sure, Western economies had always experienced the business cycle (wide swings from unemployment to inflation and back), but the nineteenth and early twentieth century economists (often called the *classical economists*) felt that an economy would automatically correct itself. It had to (they thought), because when output is produced by businesses, there must be an equivalent amount of income generated by that production. As French economist Jean Baptiste Say (1767–1832) said in his famous "Say's Law," "Supply creates its own demand."

So what did the classical economists say would happen if we suddenly experienced a significant downturn in the business cycle resulting in high unemployment? They reasoned that the unsold output would eventually force prices down. Low prices would in turn stimulate demand, and soon businesses would be rehiring the workers that had been laid off. What happened, though, if some people didn't get their jobs back?

The classical economists had a logical answer for this too. The lower wage would force cost-conscious businessmen to hire workers at lower wages. The wage rate might drop considerably, but eventually everyone would be back at work, or so the reasoning went. The classical economists thought the worst thing that could happen to this neat, self-correcting system was to allow government to interfere. In short, the bywords of the classical age might have been "stay cool and everything will take care of itself."

But then the Great Depression arrived. Something was terribly wrong. Unemployment went from bad to worse—and *stayed* that way year after year. Prices dropped, as did wages and interest rates. But there were no consumer spending sprees, and businesses didn't invest or rehire the unemployed—even at the lower wage rates. Farmers found prices so low that at times they didn't bother to haul their crops to market. Incomes in turn were so depressed that few consumers had sufficient purchasing power to buy up what was available. The nation was running out of patience: You don't "stay cool" for five years or more when you are out of work. What we needed was a new theory that worked. The time was ripe for the genius of J. M. Keynes. Let's now examine his theory in greater detail.

Keynes And The Great Depression

To fully understand Keynes's ideas, we must develop a new model of our economy. It will be something like our old demand model, but now we have to take into consideration the markets for *all* goods and services. When we talk about total supply, we mean the real GNP. As for the total demand, we are speaking of the sum of all types of spending—consumption, business investment, and government spending.

What would the total supply curve look like in our new model? Recall that our supply curve in Chapter 3 was a description of how much of one product suppliers wanted to provide at different prices. We now want that same information with respect to total supply, but this time we are dealing with the variables of spending and output instead of price and quantity.

Thus we ask the suppliers (all businesses): "If the expected amount of spending were $4 trillion, how much output (GNP) would you want to supply?" It should be obvious that if spending were at a level of $4 trillion, businesses would theoretically want to supply the *same* amount of GNP, i.e., $4 trillion (see Figure 8–3a).

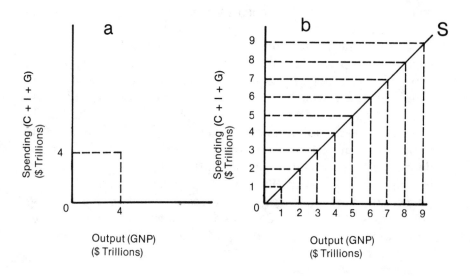

Figure 8-3

To put it differently, suppliers would only produce $4 trillion of GNP if they could be sure that it would be bought up.

All the other points on our total supply curve (see Figure 8–3b) are thus quite easy to locate. For example, if there were $8 trillion worth of spending (C + I + G), then businesses would want to supply $8 trillion worth of GNP output. In general, any amount of spending will be matched with an equivalent amount of GNP supply. Each dot on the curve is therefore in a straight line equally distant from both the output and spending axes. Our supply curve (which doesn't really curve) thus begins in the lower left corner and shoots straight up to the right on an angle of 45 degrees.

Now let's look at total demand. To draw our demand curve, we must answer the following question: "How do spenders react to changes in their income?" Let's look at an example. Suppose your individual income this year was $9,000, but next year it was reduced to $4,000? What would happen to your spending pattern for next year? Most people faced with this situation would probably spend more than the $4,000 income at least in the short run. We will say you spend $8,000 even though your income is lower. (For a while, therefore, you will be borrowing money.) This point in Figure 8–4 is in the lower left corner, representing $8,000

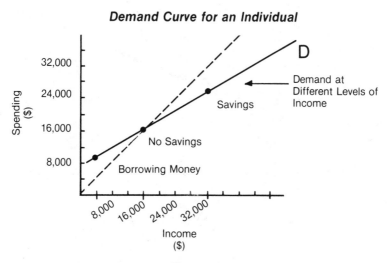

Figure 8-4

spending but only $4,000 income. Let's now move up the income scale: Your income is now $16,000, and you find that you are spending all of it. We will label this point on our demand curve "no savings." Finally, at a $32,000 income you are able to save some since you're spending only $24,000.

But what about the overall economy? Will the total demand—that is, C + I + G—have a shape similar to the demand curve in Figure 8–4? Yes. It is reasonable to assume that at low income levels we tend to spend more (at least in the short run) than our income, and as our incomes leap upward, the tendency is to save. Community spending patterns would thus be similar to patterns of individual families. Let's see now what "total supply" and "total demand" look like together (see Figure 8–5).

Note in Figure 8–5 that we have added GNP (total output) to the horizontal axis along with total income. The reader may wonder how we can equate both concepts. Are they the same?

Yes, because for every dollar's worth of output there will also be a dollar's worth of income generated. Thus, if we added up the incomes from all economic activity (wages, rents, profits, and interest), the total would be equivalent to the final value of our goods and services (GNP). Take, for example, the chair you are presently

Figure 8-5

sitting in. Isn't its final price a "summary" of all the different incomes that went into producing and distributing the chair? Thus, by definition, total incomes = GNP = total output.

Returning to our diagram of total supply and demand (see Figure 8-5), we see that there is an equilibrium level, point B, of income where aggregate supply crosses aggregate demand (just as in Chapter 3 we had an equilibrium for the supply and demand for corn). To prove that B must be the equilibrium, let's see what would happen if we were *not* at this point. What will take place at point A for example?

At point A, we find that the spending level (C + I + G) is *greater* than the amount of output produced. There can be no equilibrium under these conditions because if spending is greater than output, businesses must crank up their factories to meet the surplus demand (remember that businesses want to supply whatever is demanded). Thus at A, forces are set into motion that push output to higher levels (i.e., toward B).

The economy can't remain at point C for very long either. Here, the amount of spending is *less* than the amount of output. This situation forces producers to cut back output—GNP will go down, and soon we will return to the equilibrium point. B is the only point on our graph where production exactly matches the level of spending; hence, it is the only point of continuous stability.

We are now ready to understand John M. Keynes's great discovery. Keynes saw that an economic system might be in a *stable equilibrium at a depression level of GNP*; i.e., graphically, if supply crossed through demand at a low level of national income, the country might sit there for years and years. Classical economists talked endlessly about falling wages and falling prices in the 1930s, but these same self-regulating mechanisms never pulled us out of the worst depression in U.S. history. What was needed was a new economic policy.

Fiscal Policy

What was Keynes's prescription? If we closely study the total supply-demand graph, we should be able to see what might to be done. What is needed is to somehow "lift up" the total demand curve to an ideal point where supply crosses demand at a full employment level of GNP. Let's see how this would look on our supply-demand graph (see Figure 8-6).

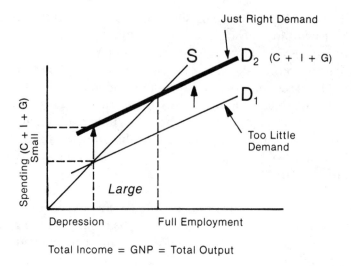

Figure 8-6

Politicians, facing unhappy citizens without jobs, are not interested in some obscure theory; they need policies that can be translated into direct action. Keynes's basic prescription for lifting the total demand curve was to have the government stimulate demand by *injecting new spending* into the economy. It can do this in two ways:

1. Increase government spending G (without altering taxes)
2. Decrease taxes (without altering government spending), thus increasing C, consumption spending

Either or both of these two *fiscal* (budgetary) policies will shift the total demand upward as can be seen in Figure 8–6.

Now look closely at the diagram in Figure 8–6. Do you notice anything unusual? A careful examination of the upward shift in demand shows that a relatively *small* increase in spending results in a *large* increase in output and incomes. For example, a $10 billion increase in government spending might result in a $20 billion (or more) increase in GNP. In short, any extra dollars spent are supercharged dollars! Economists call this the *multiplier effect*. Why are these new spending dollars multiplied? Let's look at an illustration. If, for example, the government cuts my taxes by $5, my own income will have gone up by that amount. I may spend all or part of that $5. Let's say I save $1 and spend the rest. My $4 expenditure suddenly becomes extra income for someone else, perhaps the plumber who fixed my leaky bathroom sink. The plumber, in turn, will save a little and spend the remainder, and so will the next person and the next. Now if $5 of extra spending has a supercharged effect, so will an extra $5 billion or $50 billion. Of course, this effect can work in reverse too; i.e., a $5 billion reduction in spending will obviously reduce GNP by much more than the original $5 billion.

Although the strategy to cure a recession can be rather simply stated—increase government spending and reduce taxes—the administration of these policies is another story. Any time you adjust expenditures and taxes you are tampering with the federal budget. What would the impact on our federal budget be if we lowered taxes and simultaneously increased government expenditures? We would obviously have a *deficit*, and budgetary deficits are usually considered "bad economics." Indeed in the 1930s, "spending your way into prosperity" seemed rather odd to some and even dangerous to others. The federal budget simply had to be balanced.

A serious and unfortunate occurrence, the economic disaster of the 1930s, might therefore have been avoided with federal budgetary manipulation. Even as recently as the Kennedy administration, members of congress were not totally receptive to the idea of stimulating the economy with a tax cut. However, when the Kennedy tax bill was passed in 1964 the sluggish economy steamed ahead with such speed that the taxes collected on higher incomes eventually paid back the deficit that had been incurred by the original tax cut!

It was, in fact, the spending for the Vietnam War *and* expensive social programs (of the late 1960s) plus the huge upsurge in OPEC oil prices (of the mid-1970s) that spoiled what might have been an age of real economic growth with only moderate inflation. Instead, the decade of the 1970s brought Americans a new age of high inflation.

So what would J. M. Keynes have said about inflation? What fiscal policies would now be in order? To answer this, let's take a look at the inflation problem on our total-supply-and-demand graph (see Figure 8–7). Obviously, the problem is now *too much demand*.

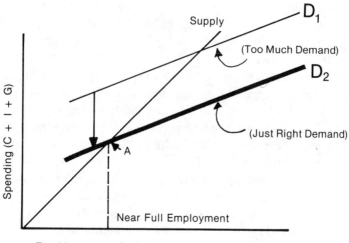

Figure 8-7

The economy is producing maximum output, but the spending level is even greater than the available GNP. It's a classic example of demand-pull inflation where "too many dollars are chasing after too few goods." Looking at the chart, we see that the demand line is intersecting with supply far above the ideal and should come down to a noninflationary equilibrium. Although we may not be able to achieve zero inflation and full employment at the same time, there is no reason why we can't try for a balance of moderate inflation and near full employment (see point A).

The correct antiinflationary prescription to pull demand down would therefore be to raise taxes, lower government spending, and generally work toward a budgetary *surplus*. Indeed, this solution seems relatively simple. So why is it so difficult to administer an antiinflationary economic policy?

To come to grips with the problem of inflation, we must understand the mysteries of the political process, since fiscal policy is ultimately decided by the President and Congress. Let's return for a moment to Keynes's prescriptions for combating unemployment. Although at one time there were some qualms about budgetary deficits, the remedies themselves—cutting taxes and increasing spending—can be almost "enjoyable" for a politician. Everyone likes a hefty tax cut, and the special interest groups—from the Army to the Peace Corps, from the poverty worker to the peanut farmer—thrive on additional spending programs. The cure for a recession then is a kind of "happy problem," because every politician from the President on down stands to gain in popularity with each new tax cut; with each new subsidized program; and, of course, with each additional worker put back on the job.

Inflation is something else, however. The economist's recommendations to increase taxes and cut back vested interest programs can be political suicide. In fact, a number of economists have concluded that the Keynesian remedies for inflation are simply inoperable because of these political realities.

Thus, up to the 1970s we could say that the Keynesian revolution in economic policy gave us a good measure of economic security. Indeed our record has been pretty good in avoiding serious economic downturns since the 1930s. Most economists felt then that unless there were new and unknown factors looming in the near future (war, global drought, world debt crisis, etc.), we would probably never live through a great depression again—thanks in large part to J. M. Keynes!

But then the 1970s arrived with an energy crunch and unacceptable rates of inflation. Suddenly Keynesian policies did not seem to be working. Not only was there political paralysis in dealing with inflation (including the failure of price-wage controls), but we were also moving toward a new era of inflation and recession combined. By the mid-1970s we were hearing the ominous word *stagflation* (stagnation + inflation) more and more, and by 1975 it was apparent that for the first time in our history, we would have inflation rates of over 8 percent combined with a bonafide recession! Some economists were advocating contractive fiscal policies to combat inflation, and others wanted just the opposite; i.e., large tax cuts to help put people back to work. In short, there were no longer any simple Keynesian remedies.

Thus, the stage was set in the early 1980s for a new approach to emerge—*supply-side economics.* Supply-side theory revolves around two key ideas that are intimately intertwined: economic incentives and economic growth. More specifically, the assumption was made that what our stagflated economy needed was not more spending stimulus but *greater incentives to improve the supply of goods and services.*

The government (under the Reagan administration) chose to encourage these incentives by *reducing overall tax rates.* The centerpiece supply-side legislation was initiated in 1981 (and reinforced in 1986) and included large, across-the-board, individual tax-rate cuts, designed to stimulate work effort and generate greater savings. It was hoped that these reforms would (in the long run) translate into more investment spending, and the additional investment plus work incentive would, in turn, enhance the nation's productivity (output/worker). Improved productivity might then moderate inflation and promote growth. Finally, the resulting growth would (according to the theory) generate such a large increase in the nation's income that the additional tax revenues would eventually pay back the short-term loss of revenue caused by the lower tax rates. If everything worked as intended, we would have a balanced budget and higher growth and productivity, but without any inflationary penalty.

Supply-side recommendations also included greater incentives for business investment, research and development, plus reducing the web of government regulation that often frustrated business activity while adding to costs. The supply-side theorists claimed that far too much attention had been paid to stimulating the demand side, to enforcing cumbersome regulations, and to evolving a tax system that discouraged saving and work effort, thus leaving the supply-side of the equation to languish with low productivity and high inflation.

Actually, supply-side economics is not an entirely new idea. We already noted Jean Baptiste Say's emphasis on supply, which he was certain would, sooner or later, "create its own demand." Also, economic philosophers David Hume (1711–1776) and Charles Montesquieu (1689–1775) warned their eighteenth-century readers that excessive tax rates would cause a diminishing work effort. In fact, no one perhaps better described the central thesis of supply-side economics better than Montesquieu, when he wrote:

> Nature is just to all mankind; she repays them for their labors; she renders them industrious because she attaches the greatest recompense to the greatest works. But if an arbitrary power snatches away the rewards of nature, one will learn distaste for work, and inactivity will appear to be the only good.[36]

Supply-side economics is thus one idea competing for attention. Recall too that there is another group of economists who look upon the future as a period of dwindling world resources and are thus skeptical about the possibility of continued economic expansion. Their ideas, in contrast to those of supply side, revolve around the question of how to rearrange the economic system so that we can be reasonably well off without the necessity for continual exponential economic growth.

At any rate, new theories eventually supersede the old. Creative and innovative ideas, combined with specific policies to deal with changing economic conditions, are continuously needed. Hence, we will always be looking for economic philosophers like an Adam Smith or a John M. Keynes—this time, however, matching wits with our own troubled times.

Chapter 9

MONEY

Choose fifty of your friends, acquaintances, or relatives and imagine that you are all shipwrecked on a large, lovely island in the middle of the South Pacific. At first, it is an idyllic life as everyone lounges on the sunny beach waiting for the rescue ship to sail into view, but after a few days you begin to realize the seriousness of your predicament. With grim faces, everyone gathers on the beach to map out some kind of survival plan.

A government is elected and soon the necessary specialized tasks are taken up by different individuals. Since Joe Jones is a carpenter, he volunteers to build thatched huts for all the families. Smith and Baker are assigned to make fishing boats and nets. Chester Olson will gather wild foods for the community larder.

Time passes. The island economy becomes more specialized and complex. Before too long, however, major problems arise as the group experiences bottlenecks in their transactions. Individuals become frustrated when they attempt to get their thatched roofs mended or to obtain food for the evening meal. What's wrong?

The problem is that our little economy has become so complex that it needs a monetary system to keep it running smoothly. The islanders are currently using *barter* for each and every exchange. This works fine on a limited scale, but add a few more skills and a few more people and the community begins to encounter some major problems.

As an example, suppose that your specific skill is mending clothing. One day you decide you would like some of Chester's fine wild foods, and you propose to trade your service for part of

Chester's stores. Unfortunately, Chester tells you he doesn't need any of his clothing mended; so what do you do? In a moneyless economy, you would have to find a third party who not only needed clothing repaired but also had a service that Chester wanted. If you couldn't find that third person, you would be out of luck.

Thus, everyone on the island begins to see the need to develop some kind of monetary supply to facilitate exchange. Money that is effectively doing its job functions as a universally accepted *medium of exchange*. It also acts as a *standard of value*. As such, the money supply has a single monetary unit (for example, a dollar) that is a common denominator for all economic goods and services. (It's really amazing, for example, that we can compare a dollar's worth of hamburger with a billion dollar nuclear reactor—both with the same unit of currency!). Finally, money can be used as a *store of value*. It can be saved or spent, hoarded or invested. It's a marvelous tool, and, without a doubt, one of mankind's most useful inventions.[37]

The islanders thus elect a banker (John Jacob Harrison III) and give him the responsibility of devising a monetary system for the island. Since John has never thought much about the characteristics of money, he forms a banking committee to discuss the issue. "Let's first list the different attributes that our new money system should have," says John as the committee sits down for a meeting. Baker then makes the first point. "Whatever we use for money must be fairly *durable* and something that can be *easily transferred* from person to person." Everyone nods in agreement.

Then after a moment's silence, Joe Jones suddenly says, "There must be a basic unit (like the dollar) that can be *divided* into smaller units as well as *multiplied* into larger units, right?" The group feels that although this is a sound point in theory, it is impractical on the island because of the limited supply of materials suitable for money.

Chester, sitting off by himself, is thinking very hard about something. He suddenly stands up and says, "Hold on, hold on. The most important thing about money is its *limited supply*—too much of the stuff will make it worthless." Everyone is impressed by Chester's insight. John (the banker) says, "You're absolutely right, Chester, but you haven't gone far enough." There is a hushed

silence as John formulates his thoughts and then continues: "Yes, our money supply must be limited, but we must also be able to *expand the amount of money in the economy as the economy itself expands.* We have a problem here because whatever we use for money must be easy for us (the authorized bankers) to duplicate, but very difficult or impossible for any unauthorized person to counterfeit. We therefore need to be quite careful of what we choose to use as money."

Baker thinks that buttons could be used. "The banking committee would need authorization to remove all the buttons from the islander's clothing. . . ." But before Baker can say another word, he is told to sit down and think of something else. Someone now suggests "shoelaces." It is argued that the laces could be cut up into different denominations. Other suggestions include everything from braided hair to pieces of paper with the banking committee's signatures. Jones remembers reading somewhere that cigarettes had been used successfully for money in the prisoner-of-war camps during World War II. The committee votes on the various suggestions and decides to try the idea of signed pieces of paper.

The last question the islanders have to face is how the committee is going to make this currency valuable. What, in fact, makes *any* currency valuable? Shifting now from our desert island illustration to the U.S. economy, we might therefore ask, "What makes our own dollar valuable?"

The U.S. Dollar

Many people are under the misconception that the dollar's value is maintained by "backing it up" with a precious metal such as gold or silver. They may be surprised to discover, however, that the last vestige of gold backing (25 percent) was removed by Congress in 1967 in order to release gold reserves for international monetary obligations.

The answer really boils down to an intangible quality that revolves around *trust.* Money is valuable because we have faith that each one of us will accept it as a legitimate medium of exchange. If all of a sudden everyone thought that money had no value, then, indeed, it would have no value. Fortunately, there is no reason for people to abandon faith in their dollars—unless, of course, the government doesn't do its job. An example of this

would be the event in which the government issued too much money. In this case, money becomes *too* plentiful, and there would be a relative shortage of things to buy. We would then experience inflation. Under extreme conditions of hyperinflation, the population might well lose faith in the government's currency and return to bartering or develop black market currencies.

On the other hand, if there is not enough money to go around, normal economic transactions would be stifled, which can also be dangerous for the economy. We need to have just the right balance between output and money in order for our dollars to remain valuable.

There was a time, however, when our citizens did not accept the legitimacy of the federal currency. The man who became our first President spoke with great fervor on this subject:

> George Washington . . . denounced those who refused to accept at full value the bills of the Continental Congress as "pests to society and the greatest enemies we have to the happiness of America. I would to God that some one of the more atrocious in each state was hung in gibbets upon a gallows five times as high as the one prepared by Haman."[38]

Faith and trust do not come automatically. They are earned by careful monetary regulation and controls. How then is the U.S. money supply controlled? A good question, yet it is one that most Americans could probably not answer correctly.

It is generally thought that our money supply is controlled simply by turning on and off the printing presses. If we want more money, the government just prints it up. This notion is only partly true since our money supply (i.e., immediately spendable assets) is more than just *currency* (bills and coins); it is also in the form of *demand deposits* or checking accounts. In fact, currently there is considerably more money in demand deposit form than in total currency. Thus, in order to control the money supply, we must be able to regulate these demand deposit dollars as well as paper currency. How is this done?

Think of the billions of dollars in checking accounts throughout the United States. Surely much of this money must be derived from a variety of credit forms such as mortgages, installment credit, and business credit. It would be reasonable to assume then that if the government could in some way *manipulate credit conditions*, it would have some control over the money supply.

Easy credit conditions usually mean more loans; more loans, in turn, mean more dollars flowing through the economy.

Thus, if the government can control credit conditions, it will not only affect the money supply, but, perhaps more importantly, it will also be able to influence the total amount of spending. This means that whoever is in charge of the money supply (through manipulating credit) can have as much power over the economic system as those who control the federal budget. We already know that the President and Congress decide on the budget, but who is responsible for regulating credit conditions and the money supply?

The Federal Reserve System

The money supply is determined and regulated in large part by our central banking system, the Federal Reserve (often called the "Fed"). In fact, if we were to pinpoint where the major decisions are made on money matters, we would zero in on the seven-man Board of Governors of the Federal Reserve System in Washington, D.C. From there we would move down to the twelve regional Federal Reserve Banks situated in major cities around the country. Take a moment now to look at a dollar bill and see from which Federal Reserve Bank it is issued (the source is written around the large letter to the left of Washington's face). Your dollar was probably issued by a Federal Reserve Bank nearby. The three bills I looked at came from Minneapolis (I), St. Louis (H), and Chicago (G).

Monetary control then flows from the twelve regional reserve banks down to the commercial banks that "belong" to the Federal Reserve System. These commercial banks (often called *member banks*) hold stock in the Federal Reserve System and are required to follow certain policies that the Fed establishes. Perhaps you know of a "First National" bank in your area; you can be sure that it is one of these member banks. However, not all banks belong to the Fed. Of all commercial banks, only about one third are members of the system. Yet those that do belong are the "workhorses" of the banking industry handling some 70 percent of all U.S. bank deposits. The question now arises as to how these commercial banks make their profits.

The profit philosophy of both member and non-member banks is simple: "Borrow money cheap, lend it dear." The difference between the rate of interest paid out for savings, checking, and other depositors' accounts and the rate of interest charged for mortgage and installment loans is the primary source of banking profits. Thus, the commercial bank's major responsibility is to take in the deposits from those who want to save and, in turn, to lend out that money to those who want to borrow. The commercial bank is what economists call a *financial intermediary*, the middle-man between savers and investors.

If the function of commercial banks is to hold deposits and to make loans, what then is the function of the regional Federal Reserve bank? The regional banks are a kind of "banker's bank." They hold deposits and make loans to member banks. The deposits are called *reserves* (hence the name Federal Reserve), and the loans are called *discounts*. The regional reserve banks also function as clearing houses for the millions and millions of checks that are sent around the country, and they also supervise the member banks in their region. Finally, the twelve regional reserve banks supply their districts with federal reserve notes (dollar bills) and other currency.

However, the real power within the Federal Reserve System— the power to influence credit and spending and ultimately unemployment and inflation—rests with the powerful Board of Governors and its various committees. How then do they go about their job of influencing the money supply, and what mysterious tools does this small band of government bankers have at its command?

We learned earlier in this chapter that the key to influencing the money supply is the control of credit. Therefore, if the Fed makes it difficult for the commercial banking system to give out loans, this should cause a slowing in the growth of the money supply. If loans are easy to obtain, the money supply will grow faster than before. What is needed then is a way to influence the loan decisions of bank officers throughout the country. To see how this is accomplished, we must first understand the concept of bank reserves.

Every bank that belongs to the Federal Reserve System must agree to set aside a certain percentage of its deposits in the form of reserves. For example, the Fed guidelines might say that your local bank must set aside at least 12 percent of its checking accounts (*demand deposits*) and 7 percent of its savings accounts (*time deposits*) as reserves. We call these percentages *reserve ratios*. Let's look at an example to see how this works.

Suppose that you live in Plum City, New York, and your newly established commercial bank, with an initial $1,000 in checking deposits, decides to join the Federal Reserve System. If the reserve ratio for checking accounts is 12 percent, then your bank must set aside a reserve of $120. After thinking about this situation, the Plum City First National Bank directors might decide that if they want to make any loans, they better have some *excess reserves* above and beyond the required $120. Do you see why?

The reason is the following: If any of the Plum City bank's customers borrow money and then cash loan checks at another bank, Plum City would lose reserves and the other bank would gain them. To explain, assume that our bank (with only $120 in reserves) just loaned Sam Smith $500. This money, of course, immediately goes into Sam's checking account. Suppose that he then takes the full $500 and spends it all out of state while vacationing in Florida. If Sam spends his money this way, there won't be sufficient funds to transfer to the Florida bank (remember that all payments between banks involve a transfer of reserves). Therefore, in order to *safely* loan Sam $500, the Plum City bank would be wise to have at least $500 in excess reserves to cover the loan.

In summary, a bank's capacity to lend out money will depend primarily on the size of its excess reserves. If there are generally large amounts of excess reserves in banks throughout the country, we will usually find *easy* money conditions, and if banks around the country are holding few excess reserves, we can then expect *tight* money conditions. We should also note here that if there are "new" dollars loaned out and therefore "new" money created, other banks will receive this additional money. They can, in turn, use this money (after putting away a fraction as required reserves) for further expansion of the money supply—something like the multiplier effect of the last chapter. Naturally, this monetary multiplier works in reverse if there is a net reduction in loans.

Monetary Policy

The obvious question we must now ask is: "Since the key to controlling credit conditions and the money supply lies in controlling excess reserves, exactly how does the Federal Reserve influence the amount of excess reserves in the overall banking system?"

One way is simply to raise or lower the reserve ratio. To use an exaggerated example, what would happen if the Fed increased the reserve ratio for checking accounts from 12 to 20 percent? Suddenly the excess reserve position (and the potential to make loans) would be diminished by billions and billions of dollars! On the other hand, if the Fed lowered the reserve ratio, the banks would have an automatic expansion of excess reserves and an easing up of credit conditions. Power over the reserve ratio is thus translated into power over the money supply.

Another monetary tool used to manipulate excess reserves is the buying and selling of government securities. U.S. commercial banks are presently holding billions of dollars worth of government obligations—bonds, notes, and other securities. The banks purchase these because they frequently offer attractive interest rates. In order to *reduce* excess reserves, all the Fed has to do is *sell* more securities to the member banks. This reduction comes about because member banks pay for the securities *by taking the money out of their reserve accounts*. The immediate lowering of these reserves thus reduces the potential loaning capacity of the commercial bank, meaning tighter money conditions throughout the economy.

What if the Fed should decide to *buy* securities from member banks? Everything that occurred above will be reversed. The money from the Fed will enlarge the reserve accounts of the banks so that more "potential" money will be available for regular loans. Buying back securities from the member banks may, therefore, result in more loans; an increased growth in the money supply; and, hopefully, more spending.

The specific group that decides whether to buy or sell securities is the *Open Market Committee*. It should be noted that these open-market operations are used more frequently than changing the reserve ratio. When the Fed changes the reserve ratio—particularly upward—it causes great hardships for banks who are "all loaned up," that is, have already lent out their maximum amount of money. The flexibility and ease of open-market operations make it the number one monetary tool of the Federal Reserve.

Our last major monetary control is called the *discount rate*. Do you remember from our earlier discussion that one of the Fed's services to member banks is a borrowing privilege? The loans that are made to member banks are called discounts, and the interest rate on these loans is thus called *discount rate*. By raising the discount rate, the Fed will discourage borrowing by member banks. Those banks who reduce the amount of money they borrow from the Fed will themselves have less money to lend out to their own customers. On the other hand, lowering the discount rate will encourage some member bank borrowing, and these banks will then have more excess reserves to meet the local demand for mortgages, installment loans, and so on. Lowering the discount rates might also *indirectly* influence other interest rates throughout the economy. For example, after hearing that the discount rate has gone down, most member banks would be inclined to "return the favor" by lowering the interest rates of their own loans. These three controls—reserve ratio, open market operations, and discount rates—are thus the monetary tools by which the Fed not only regulates the money supply but also contributes to the stabilization of the economy.

Let's now summarize what we learned about monetary policies and apply it to what we already know of supply and demand. First, inflation. If our country were facing severe inflation, the probable course of action taken by the Fed would be one, two, or all of the following, as shown in Figure 9–1:

1. To raise the reserve ratios
2. To raise the discount rate
3. To sell government securities

ANTI-INFLATIONARY MONETARY POLICY:

1. Raise Reserve Ratio
2. Raise Discount Rate
3. Sell Government Securities

(Leads to) Less Excess Reserves → Less Loans → Less Money → Higher Interest Rates

Figure 9-1

If money became very scarce, the overall interest rates might go sky high as they did in 1970, 1974, and the early 1980s. The combined impact of high interest rates and tight money conditions would probably discourage business investment spending (and also dampen consumer demand for interest-rate-sensitive durables such as autos and housing). This sequence of events as graphed in Figure 9–1, ultimately leads to a reduction in investment spending and is thus the basis of the Fed's antiinflationary monetary policies. We have come full circle; our economic controls for influencing spending are now complete.

Recall our old diagram of total supply and demand from the previous chapter. There we described the Keynesian fiscal policies that could raise or lower consumption spending (C) through changes in taxes and government spending (G). The total demand curve might rise or fall, depending on whether we were facing inflation or recession.

Now we know that monetary policies also have a profound impact on the third component of total spending: investment (I). Monetary policies that combat inflation would therefore have the following effect on our total-supply-demand diagram (see Figure 9–2).

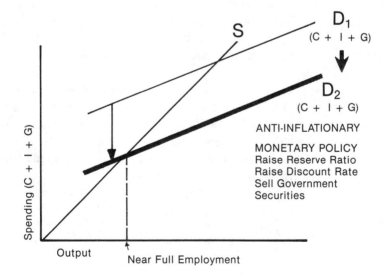

Figure 9-2

For recession, the appropriate monetary policies for easing credit conditions should be:

1. To lower the reserve ratio
2. To buy government securities
3. To lower the discount rate

In theory then, excess reserves would first increase. Then, as the money supply grew, credit would be easier to obtain. More money in the system would eventually drive interest rates down. Easier money plus low interest rates would hopefully encourage investment spending, which would, in turn, help lift up the total-demand curve.

How closely do these theories match reality? Economists are quick to point out that they are much more effective in combating inflation than recession. During an inflationary period, the monetary screws can be tightened until money and credit are actually squeezed off. In 1970 and 1981, we experienced some of the harmful side effects of ultratight money, e.g., a "depression" in the housing industry when mortgage rates were driven to unreasonable levels.

On the other hand, if we lower interest rates and make credit easily available, we cannot force more investment. For example, our depression years saw very low interest rates, yet the other negative factors, such as stock market slump, low incomes, loss of confidence, and general pessimism, far outweighed the expansionary effects of easy money.

In conclusion, whatever limitations the Federal Reserve System faces, today or in the future, it will nonetheless continue to be a critical economic institution, hopefully helping us to maintain a stable economy, a healthy commercial banking system, and, finally, a trustworthy monetary base in which we can go about our private economic affairs with a feeling of confidence.

Chapter 10

THE BENEFITS OF TRADE

It has become commonplace to hear businesspeople or economists or even government officials speak of a "global economy," to proclaim that our jobs, our markets, indeed our very material comforts are becoming more and more dependent on international arrangements. Indeed, to a certain degree, this is true. Representative of this reality is the emergence of world corporations (sometimes called *multinationals)* who, without embarrassment, take advantage of opportunitites with minimal regard or loyalty to their country of origin. Consider, for example, the following press release:

> General Motors Corp. is going to put a French name on a German car that will be built in South Korea for export to America. GM's Pontiac division will resurrect the LeMans name and put it on the subcompact economy car it begins importing next year as a 1988 model from South Korea. The car was designed by GM's West German subsidiary, Adam Opel AG, and will be built by Daewoo Group Ltd., which is 50 percent owned by GM.[39]

At the root of these changes is, of course, a growing desire for nations to engage in international trade. Perhaps then we should take a few moments to answer the very basic questions: "Why do countries like the United States, Japan, Mexico, Germany, and the U.S.S.R. trade? What's in it for them? What's in it for us? How do we benefit?" Let's examine some possible answers.

Perhaps the most obvious reason to trade is to get essential or highly desirable raw materials that cannot be obtained domestically. For example, the United States must import most of its bauxite (used in aluminum smelting), chromium, manganese, and cobalt and, to a lesser extent, oil, potash (used in fertilizer), zinc, nickel, and tin. Add to this list some nonessential (but desirable) food imports, such as coffee, tea, bananas, and cocoa, and you can begin to see how important international trade is to the United States. And what is true for us is even more true for most other countries that are less endowed with the basic raw materials for industrial production.

Another obvious benefit from trade is that it *promotes competition* in our highly concentrated industries. Consumers almost always benefit from having more choice among products as opposed to less. Imported products usually offer us more variety, sometimes better quality, and frequently lower prices. Of course this kind of international rivalry may annoy, even hurt some of our domestic industries. Yet in the end, healthy competition usually improves the consumer's overall standard of living.

Also remember that *trade is a two-way street* and thus benefits our own export industries. Consumers and businesses in foreign countries purchase tremendous quantities of American agricultural commodities as well as many of our manufactured products including computers, plastics, farm machinery, chemicals, and aircraft. When discussing the pros and cons of trade, we should never forget that approximately one out of every eight American jobs depends somehow on on healthy trade arrangements with the rest of the world.

International trade also creates a sense of *interdependence* among world nations and can have the side effect of enhancing world peace. "We need you and you need us" is the unspoken theme as a continuous flow of imports and exports ties countries together with invisible threads of mutual benefits and frequently enhanced mutual trust. Free trade among the formally antagonistic Common Market countries (Germany, Britain, France, Italy, etc.) is a good example. The "binding effect" of trade, however, is sometimes no match for the explosive forces of nationalism. The 1979 Iranian anti-Western revolution is a good illustration of where trade's mutual benefits were not able to overcome deep seated Iranian hostility and mistrust.

Mutual interdependence has sometimes been criticized as creating an unhealthy dependence, especially on critical imports, such as those related to defense. This problem is compounded when the essential import is controlled by a monopolist country (i.e., the sole supplier) or, in the case of oil, by a cartel (OPEC). Thus the huge increase in oil prices during the 1970s alerted us to the need to promote conservation and to develop our own alternative energy supplies. We should keep in mind, however, that such a monopolistic situation is unusual and should not distract us from recognizing the general benefits of free trade.

Perhaps you are still not convinced. Running through your mind may be the following thoughts: "Sure trade is a good outlet for our own surpluses and yes, it provides us with some essential raw materials; it may even create some healthy rivalry in certain industries. But what about the situation where the United States is obviously good at producing certain products, yet over a period of time we find ourselves losing out to imports at the expense of American jobs; how can you then argue that free trade is a good thing?"

It's a good question, one that is often on the minds of workers, businesses, and elected representatives. The answer, surprisingly, is, "Yes, free trade is still a positive force in the long run, even though there may be short-run difficulties." This discovery was made about 150 years ago by British economist David Ricardo, who first began to wonder about the benefits of trade as he noted a growing volume of imports and exports between his home country of Great Britain and nearby Portugal. Ricardo observed that even though both Britain and Portugal had relatively good capabilities for producing both wine and cloth, the countries still began to specialize over time, resulting in short run unemployment in the weaker industries. Ricardo intuitively felt that both countries were better off because of the new free trade arrangement. He then set out to prove his intuitive judgment, and out of these observations and analysis came his famous *theory of comparative advantage*. Let's take a closer look at his remarkable discovery.

The Theory Of Comparative Advantage

Instead of Britain and Portugal, let's see how Ricardo's theory might pertain to trade between Japan and the United States; and instead of using wine and cloth, let's use television sets and rice. I hardly need remind the reader that Japan is quite good at manufacturing TVs—because of their relatively inexpensive labor—but

what may come as a surprise is that the United States is quite efficient at producing rice (because of our relatively abundant land
and farm capital resources). In fact, rice is one of our major food
exports!

Let's assume that both countries have the capabilities to produce both products (which they do have). We could even assume
that in terms of price, Japan has a slight edge (i.e, an *absolute advantage*) in both products, and yet, as we shall see, they will both
still benefit from specialization.

To determine which country ought to produce what, we have
to examine a simplified version of each country's production possibilities (PP) curve (remember our old "guns and butter" curve from
Chapter 1?). In Figure 10–1 we have drawn a straight line PP curve
for both countries using TVs and rice.

First let's look at the United States. Notice that the domestic
trade-off is 1 for 1; i.e., if the United States wants to produce an additional ton of rice, it must give up 1 TV set. For Japan the trade-off
is 1 for 2; i.e., if the Japanese want to produce that additional ton of
rice, they must give up 2 TV sets.

Obviously each country is capable of producing both products,
but their *opportunity costs* are significantly different. For example,
we might say that rice is *relatively cheap* in the United States (costing but 1 TV set), whereas TV sets are cheap in Japan (costing but
1/2 ton of rice). Were David Ricardo looking at these data, he would
say that the United States has a *comparative advantage* in producing rice, while Japan has a comparative advantage in the production of TV sets.

Now it should be obvious that both countries have something to
gain by producing their own specialty product and trading it with
the other country. Looking first at Japan, wouldn't Japan literally
jump at the opportunity of taking 2 TVs to the United States and
getting 2 tons of rice? Recall that before trade, these 2 TVs would
be worth (domestically) only 1 ton of rice. Similarly, the United
States, in envying the Japanese domestic terms of trade, would
leap at the opportunity to take a U.S. ton of rice to Japan and get 2
TVs—a much better deal than the 1 for 1 U.S. trade-off. But now
you're probably wondering: "Hmmm, there's something wrong
here; exactly what advantage would there be to having each country make exchanges using their own internal trade-off ratios? For

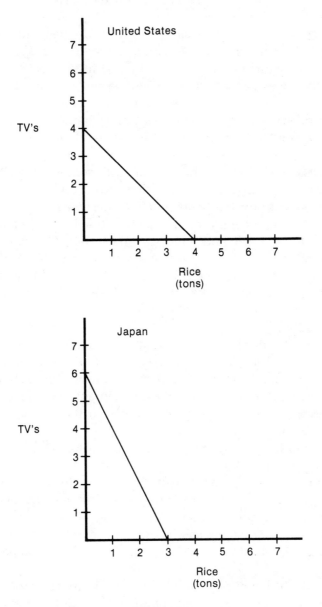

Figure 10-1

example, what's in it for the United States if it gives Japan the *same* terms of trade (1 for 1) that it can get for itself without trade . . . and vice versa?"

Were Ricardo here to consider this situation, he would probably say, "Why not compromise with some international terms of trade, i.e., something between 1 for 1 and 1 for 2." A likely candidate for the compromise (depending on the demand for each product) would be perhaps 1 ton of rice for 1½ TV sets (or the equivalent ratio of 2 rice for 3 TVs). Now the United States can take 2 tons of rice and get 3 TVs (better than 1 for 1!), while Japan need give up only 3 TVs (instead of 4) to get its 2 tons of rice.

We'll assume that both countries find this compromise satisfactory, thus obtaining some very positive end results. For example, the United States now has the potential to increase its total TV consumption by 50 percent (note that if the United States wanted to export all its rice, it could import as many as 6 TV sets), while Japan's total rice potential has increased by 33 percent (i.e., if it exported all the TVs, it could enjoy as much as 4 tons of rice instead of the original 3). These new trade possibilities can be shown on an *expanded production possibilities curve* for both countries (see Figure 10–2).

An expanded PP curve means that the consumers in each country have the opportunity to enjoy *more* of both products. Their standard of living has indeed improved, but not through an enlargement of the resource base; they are simply using the original resources more efficiently by specializing in those areas where they have a comparative advantage.

For David Ricardo, free trade gave countries this unexpected bonus. He was therefore not saddened when he saw the British cloth industry grow at the expense of its wine industry, nor did he think it unfortunate when the cloth industry in Portugal declined and wine production expanded. Though certainly causing short-run dislocations (unemployment, bankruptcies, etc.), the net long-run change was positive as each country pursued its comparative advantage.

Actually, the benefits of international trade are really no different than the benefits from trade of any kind. Think, for example, about the obvious advantages of trade within the United States. There is a significant difference, however, between international

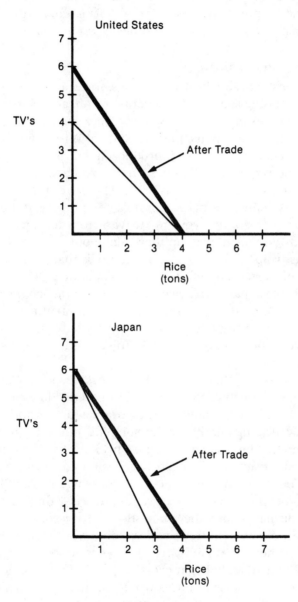

Figure 10-2

trade and domestic trade in that the dislocations caused by foreign imports are usually a *more potent political issue* than the dislocations caused by purely domestic trade. This issue, in turn, brings us to the heart of a very sensitive subject—*protectionism*.

Trade Protectionism

One of the best ways to illustrate the pressures to restrict imports (but without losing sight of the benefits from trade) is to draw up an exaggerated example involving trade between two states.

Imagine that once upon a time the state of Wisconsin was like a small, self-reliant country; i.e., it produced most, if not all its essential economic requirements. Let's further assume Wisconsinites had an unusual craving for citrus fruits. Thus, over the years there grew up in Wisconsin a thriving orange and grapefruit industry.

Perhaps at this point you might want to interrupt and ask, "How could Wisconsin, way up there along our northern border, grow citrus fruits?" The answer, of course, is that if the domestic demand were great enough (i.e., the people of Wisconsin were willing and able to pay high prices for citrus fruit), then it would be profitable to grow oranges and grapefruit in artificially heated greenhouses. Let's say that fruits grown under these conditions would have to be priced around $3 for an orange and $4 for a grapefruit.

Now let's assume that once Wisconsin established its large and thriving citrus industry, some enterprising individual discovered that the state of Florida could grow an orange for 10¢ and a grapefruit for 15¢. Adding another 5¢ for shipping, our entrepreneurial friend found that he could make a good profit selling these fruits in Wisconsin at a fraction of the old Wisconsin industry prices.

It does not take any imagination to guess what would happen after the "cheap imports" began rolling in. First there would be shock and dismay among the "domestic" (i.e., Wisconsin) growers. Undoubtedly a powerful trade association would be formed (very likely called the Wisconsin Citrus Growers Association *WCGA*) that would immediately begin exerting political pressures to help save the industry. Horror stories would circulate concerning corporate bankruptcies, loss of tax revenues, and long unemployment lines. Soon the political machinery would begin to respond by undertaking measures to promote Wisconsin fruit consumption and to discourage the importation of Florida fruit.

The first measures would probably take the form of *nontariff barriers*, subtle methods of dealing with the import problem without resorting to the more common tariffs and quotas. For example, in the beginning there might simply be massive advertising campaigns praising the virtues of "domestically" grown fruits—with perhaps the implication that some of the "cheap Florida imports" have been found to be unhealthy. We'll assume, however, that the Wisconsin consumer finds "imported" fruits just as tasty and wholesome as the home grown variety. Possibly the next tactic might be to pass a law stating that all imported fruits must be colored a dark blue. But even that strategy doesn't work—the price is simply too good!

Sooner or later the Wisconsin growers will probably convince their legislators to take more drastic steps such as setting tariffs and quotas. We will be examining these measures in greater detail, but first let's take a look at what we learned about the real world from this example.

The first lesson is that cheap imported products will almost always bring some degree of economic suffering to those industries directly affected. From the perspective of the workers, assertions of "comparative advantage" give little comfort to those workers who have lost their livelihood and incomes. Their first reaction is almost always shock, then perhaps intense anger. Consider the following story from a St. Paul, Minnesota, newspaper:

> Workers at the Teledyne Wisconsin Motor firm, which was playing host to Japanese businessmen, hauled down a Japanese flag in front of the plant and raised an American flag on the same pole.
>
> They sang the "Star-Spangled Banner" as the American banner was raised.
>
> One worker tried to burn the Japanese flag but could not ignite it. He then slashed it with a pocket knife, took it across the street and shoved it down a sewer opening.
>
> John Claffey, president of Local 283 of the United Auto Workers, said . . . the transfer of the so-called Wisconsin Robin engine business to Japan had cost "50 percent of our engine business" and that 350 people had been laid off at the West Milwaukee plant as a result.[40]

These intense feelings are understandable. Compasssion tells us that workers adversely affected by sudden shifts in international trade arrangements need help: not so much help through

protectionist measures but, instead, help in softening the pain of sudden unemployment and in aiding workers and businesses to shift their skills and resources to new industries where they have a comparative advantage.

This point brings us to the second lesson from our illustration. It should be clear that despite the economic hardship, Wisconsin really *has no business growing grapefruit and oranges.* Its land, resources, climate, etc., are far more ideal for producing dairy products. Once their specialization takes hold and Wisconsin begins to trade dairy products for inexpensive Florida citrus fruits, it's obvious that both Wisconsin and Florida will be able to enjoy a higher standard of living compared with the days before trade.

Thus the most productive reaction to the import threat would be for Wisconsin to start promoting a dairy industry. To facilitate this change, it may be necessary for the state government to offer temporary low-cost loans for certain types of farm investments, to set up research facilities, or to help seek out potential markets for dairy products. Indeed, it would be folly to attempt to hold onto the citrus production at all costs. Such a reaction *would lock Wisconsin's resources into the wrong industry for years and years.*

Strong protectionist reflexes are, however, far more common than attempts to adjust to new economic realities. We therefore need to take a closer look at the nature of these restrictions, to see how they work and how they affect the consumer.

Tariffs And Quotas

Certainly the most common strategy for fending off imports is to levy a *tariff.* This is nothing more than putting a tax on a specific imported good. Although a tariff is sometimes justified by the claim that it will generate tax revenues, the real intent is almost always to choke off foreign competition. Indeed if revenues were the issue, there would be no point in discriminating against only foreign manufacturers and levying such taxes just on them.

The economic effect of a tariff is the same as that of putting an excise tax on any product; i.e., *it lifts* the supply curve precisely the amount of the tax. How much would the consumer get hurt? That depends upon the demand elasticity as shown in Figure 10–3.

In illustration (a) we see a fairly elastic demand for Mexican tomatoes and in (b) is an inelastic situation for Canadian natural gas. In each example we have moved the supply curve a vertical distance the amount of the tariff—50¢ per unit. But because of the different elasticities, the tariff on the tomatoes increases the final price to the consumer only slightly while the same tariff for natural gas translates into a large price increase. The explanation for this can be traced to the fact that imported tomatoes are a "non-necessity" product, and there are also substitutes in the form of

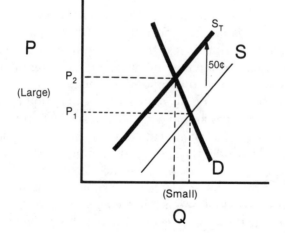

Figure 10-3

other vegetables. Natural gas, however, is definitely a necessity with few substitutes. The consumer, therefore, has no choice but to absorb most of the 50¢ tariff.

Perhaps of even greater concern to the domestic industry (the one who pushed for the tariff in the first place) is how the tariff affects the quantity of imports. In the tomato market (with elastic demand) the import "choking-off" effect is obviously greater than in the inelastic natural gas market. Generally speaking, we can say that *the greater the elasticity of demand, the more a tariff will help the domestic industry achieve its goal of keeping out foreign competition.* When the tariff approach is not effective, however, a second and more extreme protectionist strategy can be used. It's called the *quota.*

The import quota simply puts a physical limit on the quantity of imports. There is no worrying about cheap goods "flooding" the domestic market because only so much is legally allowed to enter the country. The impact of a quota can be seen in Figure 10–4.

Although economists dislike protectionist measures in any

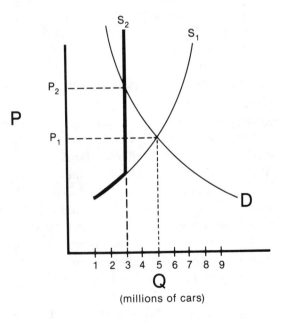

Figure 10-4

guise, they perhaps dislike quotas most of all. At least with a tariff, it is possible to get additional quantities of a product if you're willing to pay the tax. But the quota is an *absolute barrier* once the legal limit has been reached. In the example in Figure 10–4, the foreign car quota was set at 3 million, whereas the normal trade equilibrium would have been 5 million. Also notice that the restricted supply (S_2) forces those who want the product to bid the price up from P_1 to P_2. Note that when faced with quotas, some exporters simply *upgrade* their exported product; i.e., sell only the most expensive (and thus the most profitable) units, thus unfairly shutting out many lower income families from the benefits of trade.

Indeed, if there is one thread running throughout this discussion, it is that protectionist measures usually hurt consumers of all types and ultimately diminish the efficient use of world resources. Yet we still continue to use them.

A major reason for this is, of course, the sheer political power of those workers and businesses that are affected by foreign competition (recall the Wisconsin citrus-growers example). What is sometimes difficult to understand, however, is when the *public itself* expresses some of these seemingly "logical" arguments for trade restriction. We will now examine some of the arguments that are most frequently put forth by both the vested interest groups and the general public.

Arguments For Trade Protectionism

A friend once said to me (quite sincerely I believe) that we ought to restrict foreign imports because it's important "to keep our money in the country." This argument has an irrefutable ring to it—how could we *not* want to keep our dollars at home?

Upon further reflection, though, it actually doesn't make any sense. Indeed, my friend should recognize that trade is a "two-way street"; that is, our dollars that go to Japan for V.C.R.s or Toyotas come right back to us when the Japanese buy our rice, soybeans, computers, real estate, or stocks and bonds. Thus, if there is a healthy trade arrangement between countries, our money *will* eventually return to us because the Japanese have little use for dollars at home.

Another argument I hear quite often is that we ought to restrict imports because American workers cannot compete with "cheap foreign labor." This is a powerful, often emotionally charged argument—one that shouldn't be dismissed lightly. What it is saying, of course, is that products from low wage countries jeopardize American wage rates, American businesses, and ultimately, American jobs.

Those who use this argument often overlook the fact that U.S. wages are higher than wages in other countries primarily *because U.S. workers are generally more productive*; are probably better educated and more skilled; and, more often than not, use more advanced production techniques. Other less technologically advanced countries have, in fact, sometimes argued for tariffs to protect *their* domestic industries from the "unfair competition" of the "highly productive" American industrial worker or farmer.

Of course there may be certain industries where our wage rates might be out of line with industry's general level of worker productivity. But why should the American consumer be forced, through protectionist import restrictions, to subsidize high American wage rates not matched by corresponding productivity? Or putting it slightly differently, why shouldn't U.S. consumers be allowed to *benefit* from inexpensive products made by low-wage workers? And, of course, why shouldn't foreign consumers benefit from our most efficient industries?

If you scratch beneath the surface of the cheap foreign labor argument you usually discover that it is an oblique admission that a particular industry is no longer efficient according to world standards. In certain cases, some of the producers may not have modernized their factories; in other industries it may be that the wages are out of line with productivity or that product design or quality may not have kept up with foreign competition. Indeed, it would be unusual if we didn't see some domestic industries (or individual companies) lose their competitive advantage over time.

Needless to say, if we begin to erect trade barriers on the cheap foreign labor argument, there is no reason why other countries whose own industries are hurt by U.S. products cannot *retaliate* with their own tariffs and quotas on *our* products. This would be the beginning of a destructive trade restriction war where, in the end, everybody loses out. A good illustration of such shortsightedness was the enactment of the Smoot-Hawley tariffs in 1930, which raised the average cost of imported goods about 60 percent. Retaliation ensued, and the inevitable retrenchment in world trade made the great depression of the 1930s just that much worse.

The popularity of each of these seemingly "logical" arguments should not mask the fact that they simply do not hold up under scrutiny. But perhaps you're wondering, "Are there *any* conditions that might warrant interference with free trade?"

The answer to this question is a qualified "maybe." There are times, for example, when we are confronted with a violation of international morality in which restrictions on both imports and exports may be justified on *ethical grounds*. The United States, for example, once refused to import products from white supremacist (preindependent) Rhodesia. And in the late 1970s, President Carter placed an embargo on grain exports to the Soviet Union after their invasion of Afghanistan. This sanction, however, was later rescinded by President Reagan because of political pressure from American farmers.

It has also been argued that Third World countries should temporarily restrict imports so that new industries have an opportunity to become established; this is usually referred to as the *infant industry argument*. The implications here are that (1) it is desirable for the less developed countries to diversify their internal economies and (2) temporary restrictions are needed so that the "infant" can have breathing space to "mature," that is, grow efficient by world standards, without getting clobbered by the existing international giants. For this argument to be valid, the domestic industry should be forewarned that the import protection will be cut off at some specific date. Otherwise, the "infants" will probably want to perpetuate their protected status. Like the proverbial son who refuses to leave home, it's equally true that some protected industries also resist confronting the real world.

Finally, we might argue for temporary protectionist measures to prevent a genuine "culture shock" in some developing countries. Not so much an economic argument as an anthropological one, this point of view recognizes the potential for destroying traditional handicraft societies when there is a sudden, unexpected influx of machine made goods. When such an influx occurs, it frequently affects not only the economic livelihood but also the age-old cultural fabric of the community. Again, this is not an argument for permanent restrictions but simply an admission that it may be desirable to slow things down so people have a chance to make adjustments.

But when the exceptions are noted and acknowledged, the fact remains that free trade is, more often than not, a worthwhile goal. And, fortunately, the world's major trading partners generally recognize this fact. Since 1947 we have witnessed an attempt to significantly reduce trade barriers through the General Agreements for Tariffs and Trade. By the early 1980s various milestones of tariff negotiations (the so-called Kennedy Round in 1967 and Tokyo Round in 1979) reduced tariffs to historically low levels. Of course there will always be domestic pressures to impose protective tariffs and quotas, and hence there will always be the threat of a worldwide restrictive trade war lurking in the background. We should be on our guard.

Yet even without a trade war, there are still some knotty problems facing each and every country in the form of periodic imbalances of trade. It's now time to take a closer look at the age-old struggle of how countries balance their international payments.

Chapter 11

THE PROBLEMS
OF TRADE

Do you remember our fanciful story from the previous chapter about Wisconsin trading with Florida? One of the key ideas of this illustration was to show that the principles of specialization and comparative advantage apply equally to *any* kind of trade—between states, between regions, between countries. Why then do we seem to have more headaches with our trading arrangements in the international sphere than we do in the domestic realm? This question leads us to one of the most interesting issues in economics—the *balance-of-payments* problem.

Consider again Wisconsin and Florida. If it should happen that Wisconsin imports more from Florida than it exports, we might say that Wisconsin is experiencing a so-called "unfavorable" balance of trade. Yet, as noted above, nobody gets very excited about it. Why not?

It's simply because the entire United States *uses the same currency*. Thus, if Florida businesses collect a *surplus* of Wisconsin dollars, they can easily spend them in Florida—or for that matter anywhere in the United States. In the case of an unfavorable balance of trade with Japan, however, the Japanese will accumulate extra dollars that, generally speaking, cannot be spent in Japan. If this imbalance continues, the Japanese may decide it is simply no longer worth it for them to trade with us. Thus, unlike the trade between individual states, trade between countries ought to roughly "balance out" over time; otherwise the surplus country will build up quantities of unwanted foreign currencies at the expense of sacrificing real goods and services. What mechanisms or policies are available to bring an imbalanced situation back into balance?

There have, in fact, been three major approaches to dealing with this situation. The earliest solution to trade imbalances is called the *Classical Gold-Flow Model* originally described by philosopher-economist David Hume in 1752. Let's therefore begin by taking a look at Hume's theory.

Classical Gold Flow

In order for the classical model to work, Hume assumed that all the countries involved in trade had to be on an *international gold standard* and also on a *domestic gold standard.*

When trading countries go on an international gold standard, it means that traders from a foreign country who wind up with a surplus of dollars have the right to trade those dollars for American gold. If, on the other hand, traders from the United States wind up with a trade surplus, they would have the right to obtain foreign gold for their surplus currencies.

To be on a domestic gold standard means that every dollar in circulation must be redeemable or backed up by an equivalent value of gold. A country's money supply will therefore depend on how much gold it has. If the United States loses some of its gold to a foreign country, we will then be forced to reduce our domestic money supply because of a lack of gold to back it up. On the other hand, if we enlarge our gold holdings, it would automatically increase the money supply.

Before this model could begin solving a balance-of-payments problem, one further assumption needs to be spelled out: the linkage between money and prices through the so-called *Quantity Theory of Money*. This theory can be summarized quite neatly in the equation:

$$MV = PQ$$

where M equals the money supply, V the velocity of money (the number of times an average dollar changes hands during the year), P the general price level, and Q the physical volume of goods and services.

Classical economists like Hume assumed that both V and Q remain relatively constant *leaving M and P to rise or fall together.*

Thus if the U.S. money supply goes up, it drives prices up too (inflation), or if M goes down, it lowers the price level (deflation). Of course, in our simplified classical world all prices are assumed to have total flexibility, moving downward or upward with equal ease.

The stage is now set for solving an imbalance problem. Assume the United States suddenly finds itself in a serious trade deficit with Japan (U.S. imports greater than exports). As a result, Japanese receive more dollars than they can spend. Under the classical assumptions outlined above, Japanese traders exchange their surplus dollars for American gold, and the quantity of gold in the U.S. treasury falls. A reduction in our gold stock forces a reduction in the money supply. If M goes down, we can soon expect a decrease in our prices. Falling U.S. prices, in turn, make our products less expensive and therefore more attractive to the Japanese. As U.S. exports expand, we find ourselves moving toward a balance-of-payments equilibrium.

We should also note what's going on in Japan. Japan's growing gold stock means more money circulating in their economy. More money (given a fixed Q) will create Japanese inflation. Finally, high Japanese prices will discourage Japanese imports to the United States, which again helps resolve the original imbalance of payments. A summary of the relevant linkages leading to a trade equilibrium can be seen in Diagram 11A.

Classical gold flow is a neat system, completely automatic and totally reliable. It's an extremely attractive model operating like some self-regulating Newtonian machine that's continually moving the system toward a favorable equilibrium without messy maintenance or outside tinkering. So why don't we use this system today?

First, we are no longer on an international gold standard, nor is our domestic money supply backed by gold (the last vestige of backing went out in 1967). There is simply not enough total gold available to keep up with expanding domestic money supplies and the general expansion in world trade.

More important, though, even if we were on the gold standard, prices would probably not respond with the classical flexibility needed to make the system work. Today, prices tend to go up and up, very rarely down. In fact, the only time the United States has experienced general deflation in the twentieth century was during

Diagram 11A

the great depression of the 1930s. If a depression is what it takes to get prices down, it's simply not worth it. Indeed, there must be a better way to solve our international balance-of payments problem. This brings us to our second method—a method which in many ways is even simpler than the Classical model. It's called the *flexible exchange rate system.*

Flexible Exchange Rates

The key to understanding flexible exchange rates is to realize that the world's currencies are subject to supply and demand markets not unlike the markets for corn or soybeans. In theory we could draw a demand curve and a supply curve for every country's currency. Perhaps it would be helpful to illustrate this point by choosing one specific currency—the German mark.

We begin by asking the following question: "Why would Americans demand German marks?" There is basically one answer: having a supply of marks will allow us to purchase German products. Thus, the demand for marks will reflect the demand for German imports. If we should suddenly want lots more German cars or cameras, we would therefore need more marks, and hence the demand for that currency would rise.

The second question to ask is: "Why would the Germans want to supply us with marks?" Germany will supply us with marks according to their desire to purchase U.S. products. Thus, if Germans want a lot more American wheat or computers, then the supply curve for marks will increase.

Assuming that there is an equilibrium between German and American trade, there will also be an equilibrium in the market for marks. This example is illustrated in Figure 11–2.

In the market shown in Figure 11–2, we find that the "price" of a German mark (i.e., its *exchange rate*) to be 25¢. We are assuming that at the 25¢ price trade between the United States and Germany is in balance.

Now let's see what happens when Americans suddenly want a lot more German products or perhaps decide to travel more in Germany. We might also be interested in building U.S. owned factories in Germany or in increasing the number of American troops stationed there. Each of these measures will contribute to a short-run U.S. *balance-of-payments deficit* because these actions increase

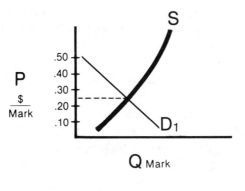

Figure 11-2

our demand for German marks. We will assume that Germany is not particularly interested in more American products; thus their willingness to supply marks remains constant. The market for marks is then altered as the demand increases in relation to a constant supply curve. This change is shown in Figure 11–3.

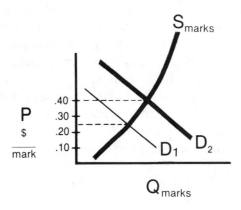

Figure 11-3

What is happening, of course, is that those who want additional marks *must bid up the price* in order to get them. This is shown by a new equilibrium price of 40¢ versus the old price of 25¢. As the price for marks goes up, we say the dollar is being *depreciated*; i.e., our dollars are now worth less in relation to German marks.

In the word *depreciation*, we discover the real key to this particular system. Since the dollar is now worth less, it will take *more* of
them to buy a given amount of German goods and services. If a bottle of German beer costs 1 mark, it now means that Americans
must pay 40¢ for that bottle as opposed to the old price of 25¢.
Virtually every economic dealing with Germany will cost more
proportionately—buying a Mercedes Benz, traveling to Bonn,
building a soap factory in Cologne, or stationing troops in Berlin.
As dollars depreciate relative to the mark, Americans should then
begin to cut back their German purchases, travel plans, etc., thus
bringing trade into balance again.

Note that the change in the currency's equilibrium price is not
only depreciation for the U.S. dollar, it's also *appreciation* for the
German mark. Germany now sees U.S. exports as less expensive (1
mark, for example, will buy 40¢ worth of U.S. goods instead of 25¢)
and therefore will begin to increase their purchase of U.S. products. They may also start to set up factories in the United States
and perhaps travel more to the United States. All of these activities
ought to help regain the original trade balance.

Since the early 1970s we have approximated this flexible exchange rate system. In fact, the illustration cited above (the depreciation of the dollar in relation to the mark) took place during the
1970s and brought about many of the changes that were outlined.
Thus the flexible system (with some minor modifications) is working today to help realign world currencies that get out of kilter.
Before we discuss current economic policies, we should take a look
at the third method of dealing with world balance-of-payments
problems: the *modified gold-fixed exchange rate system*, which
dominated the international scene for almost thirty years. How did
this system differ from the classical gold-flow model or flexible
exchange rates? Let's take a look.

Modified Gold-Fixed Exchange Rates

The fixed exchange system began at a specific time and in a specific location. It's birthplace was Bretton Woods, New Hampshire,
and the year was 1944.

It was a time when World War II was fast coming to a close.
The war had devastated much of Europe and almost all of Japan.
Entire economic infrastructures (factories, roads, power plants,
etc.) were literally blown apart.

The United States, however, was stronger than ever. Its infra-structure had remained intact; its work force was basically un-harmed. It was not surprising, therefore, that the major industrial countries of the world looked to the United States for postwar assistance and leadership.

Assistance was offered in the form of the *Marshall Plan* and the *International Bank for Reconstruction and Development*. Both of these programs poured billions of dollars into European recon-struction. As for international leadership, it was agreed at the 1944 Bretton Woods Conference that the world was henceforth to be on a *fixed exchange rate system* using the dollar as the centerpiece cur-rency. This meant that all the other major world currencies were pegged at some fixed value in relation to the dollar, and the dollar in turn, would be pegged to gold at a fixed rate of $35 per ounce. We were therefore on a *modified gold standard*: those with a sur-plus of dollars could, if they wished, trade them for U.S. gold. Still, most countries preferred to keep their dollars as reserves in their international "checking accounts." Dollars were, therefore, a kind of world legal tender. These monetary relationships can be seen in Figure 11–4.

Fixed exchange rates had the virtue of inviolable stability— backed by gold, a strong dollar, and an unrivaled American econ-omy. The chance, however, that a country might experience balance-of-payment difficulties still existed. Anticipating such problems, the Bretton Woods officials agreed to set up a fund that could loan deficit countries the requisite amount of dollars (or other currencies) as the need arose. It would be called the *Inter-national Monetary Fund* (IMF), and its chief purpose was to help make these short-term loans or perhaps to help make long-term readjustments in a country's basic exchange rate.

Suppose, for example, that some country (for example, Great Britain) kept running chronic balance-of-payments deficits. The British pound (£) then would thus be "overvalued" in relation to other currencies and would eventually have to be devalued. How would Britain devalue? British bankers would approach the IMF and *request* a new (lower) exchange rate in relation to the dollar; instead of $2.60 per pound, they might want to go down to say $2.00.

This might sound like a case of depreciating under the flexible system discussed earlier, but there are a couple of important

Figure 11-4

differences. First, the flexible system described earlier adjusts *automatically* to short-run changes in the supply and demand for a currency. In the case of the pound's devaluation, the British *had to ask the IMF for permission to devalue.* The IMF Board of Directors thus ensure orderly readjustments in world exchange rates.

The second difference is perhaps more subtle. After devaluation, the British pound is worth less not only in relation to the dollar but also to *all* other currencies, since the dollar is the major currency by which all the others are valued (see Figure 11–4). To review, depreciation means your currency has been reduced in value with *one* other currency, while devaluation reduces its value in relation to *all* currencies.

In general, the fixed exchange rate system worked reasonably well. Yet there was one major flaw: *its overwhelming reliance on the dollar.* For example, what would happen if the United States began to notice *its own* chronic balance-of-payments deficits, i.e., if the dollar itself became overvalued? How would you like to be holding millions of dollars in your international "checking account," believing these dollars would always be worth so much in terms of other currencies (as well as gold), and then, all of a sudden—pow!—have the United States devalue the dollar? This could be done by simply raising the dollar's par value with gold from $35 an ounce to say $70. The value of your dollars—those you've been holding onto with great faith—would suddenly be cut in half. The fixed exchange rate system thus had a structural inability to effectively deal with the possible devaluation of the dollar.

For a long time, however, devaluation wasn't necessary. As indicated earlier, postwar Europe was hungry for U.S. consumer goods and industrial products and therefore wanted lots of U.S. dollars. However, beginning in the mid-1950s and continuing into the 1960s, U.S. trade turned toward problematic deficits year after year.

One quite predictable reason for this was that eventually the Europeans and Japanese would begin to close the "productivity gap" that existed after the war. Their bombed-out infrastructures were, in fact, replaced with the most modern facilities available. Also, the U.S. productivity growth rate fell from a relatively high 3 percent increase per year (the average rate from 1948 to 1966) down to 2 percent (1966 to 1973). And for the rest of the 1970s, we averaged only about 1 percent per year! Not only were Japan's and Germany's productivity growing at a faster pace than ours, but some of the other energetic Asian economies, such as Taiwan, South Korea, and Hong Kong, were expanding their own export production and thus began making significant inroads into U.S. markets.

An additional problem was our relatively high inflation rate that worsened during the mid-1960s. Higher U.S. prices will, of course, tend to discourage foreign buyers and hurt our balance of payments. U.S. military presence overseas was another net outflow of dollars. In addition, the costly Vietnam War undoubtedly contributed to American inflation and trade deficits as well.

Another development that diminished U.S. exports was the formation of the European Economic Community (i.e., the *Common Market*), which promoted free trade within Common Market borders but often set up barriers to the rest of the world (including the United States). For Americans to compete, it was often necessary to make direct investments within the Common Market countries, which meant setting up our own factories on European soil. Such direct investments again contribute to a net outflow of dollars and hurt our balance of payments.

Each of these problems added to larger and larger U.S. deficits. Of course, the modified gold-fixed exchange rate system did have some techniques (short of devaluation) for coping with the problem. First, it was possible to exchange gold for the surplus dollars (as originally intended under the Bretton Woods agreement). Recall that the United States agreed to sell gold to foreign monetary authorities at the fixed rate of $35 an ounce. And indeed there were countries, like France and Austria, who often insisted on gold for their dollars. Exchanging gold, however, had its limitations because of the total U.S. gold stock. Originally worth some $25 billion right after the war, our gold reserves had shrunk to less than half that amount approximately two decades later.

Some people in Congress were tempted to solve the imbalance problem by restricting foreign goods. In the last chapter we saw that such protectionist policies were self-defeating and could easily set off a restrictive trade war. Fortunately, their plans didn't get very far. Legislators did pass laws that helped to a certain degree. Efforts to "tie" foreign aid, i.e., require that the aid recipient country purchase U.S. products were instituted. We also tried to restrict the amount of imported goods that an American tourist could bring back duty free. Again, these and other legislative efforts did not really solve the basic problem of an overvalued dollar, and yet we didn't want to devalue unless we absolutely had to.

Perhaps the easiest way to deal with the deficits was to *convince foreign monetary authorities to hold onto their surplus dollars.* We mentioned earlier that dollars became a kind of world legal tender. Many countries kept dollars strictly for this purpose; others wanted interest bearing dollar assets. Thus, if our interest rates were relatively high compared with interest rates on alternative investments, foreigners might be in no hurry to make gold exchanges.

These techniques, in addition to selling gold and arranging for assistance from the IMF, helped the United States hang on to the

Bretton Woods' system through the 1960s. But by the early 1970s, foreign dollar claims were skyrocketing, U.S. gold was dwindling to an all-time low, and still our balance-of-payments deficits continued to grow. It was obvious something had to be done or risk an international dollar crisis. The Bretton Woods fixed exchange rate philosophy was simply not compatible with the current international trade realities.

The dramatic moment finally came on the 15th of August 1971 when President Nixon suspended all gold transactions. In effect, the old system of gold convertibility went out the window. The dollar was now allowed to float, and its future value was to be determined primarily by the forces of supply and demand. By 1973 the dollar had become significantly depreciated against most of the world's major currencies. Prices of many imports—from German VWs to Japanese Datsuns, from Middle East oil to Swiss watches— all went up accordingly. No longer was the dollar in great international demand, no longer was it the paragon currency of the world. A new era had arrived.

Of course the flexible exchange rate system of the 1970s and 1980s didn't solve all our balance-of-payment problems. Various governments (including the United States) were not shy about intervening against speculators and other "threats" to their currencies, preventing at times proper currency realignments. The United States also found itself hurt by the emergence of an effective world oil cartel (OPEC) whose sudden increase in the price of crude oil in the mid-1970s contributed to a large net outflow of dollars.

Then in the first half of the 1980s, the United States witnessed something new—and to a large degree unanticipated—i.e., a phenomenal *increase* in the dollar's average exchange value against most major foreign currencies. Economists attribute this development to strong foreign dollar demand *for investments* in the United States. Why did this take place?

For one thing, the United States appeared to be a "safe haven" in a world of political uncertainty. Also, foreigners felt there were good investment opportunities, especially in the years of relatively high U.S. GNP growth. And finally, due to ebbing U.S. inflation, high real interest rates made many American investments that much more attractive. Unfortunately this large increase in the dollar's international value hurt many of our traditional exporting industries and thus contributed to large deficits in our balance-of-payments merchandise accounts.

Perhaps the most dramatic outcome of these developments was the fact that during 1985, the United States officially became a net "debtor nation" meaning that the value of foreign investments (i.e., stocks, bonds, government securities, real estate, bank deposits, etc.) in the United States exceeded our own investment in other countries. These foreign investments may indeed put the United States in a potentially more vulnerable position—especially if our "debtor" status progressively worsens. Such a development would increase the possibility (and perhaps probability) of large, even violent, currency readjustments that would be beyond our control. Sudden currency adjustments could, in turn, dramatically (and adversely) impact inflation and even jeopardize real growth and employment.

Still, it could be argued that when taking a larger view, U.S. international economic arrangements were not so bad. First, unlike some European and Asian countries, the United States is not quite so dependent on the foreign trade sector, producing approximately 85 percent of the domestically consumed goods and services here at home. (Even in the area of oil, the United States demonstrated a surprising ability to conserve and develop alternative energy arrangements. In the early 1980s one could hardly pick up a popular magazine without noticing articles on energy conservation, underground housing, fuel efficient cars, and the like.)

Also, the United States is still generally competitive in many of its traditional export industries including chemicals, soft drinks, paper products, aircraft, telecommunications, food and fiber, insurance, office machines, banking, farm machinery, computers, TV programming, just to name a few. Finally, we should recognize that even though U.S. productivity growth has slowed significantly, the American output per worker hour (in absolute terms) is still higher than most other industrialized countries.

In summary, the United States will continue to face various international trade problems in the future, and if certain trends (such as deficits and low productivity growth) become chronic problems, we will be courting trouble in future decades. Yet in relation to those nations where the majority of people live—the Third World countries—we are very well off indeed. Perhaps now it is time to leave our American shores and make a visit to these struggling nations. What is life like in these developing countries? Even more important, what does the future have in store for them?

Chapter 12

STAGNATION AND CHANGE

In the summer of 1974, well-fed Americans didn't seem quite so hostile to the high food prices as they had been the previous year. One explanation might have been the horrifying stories in the major news magazines and on television—horror stories not just of high food prices but of no food at all. During that summer there was very little food for millions of North Africans suffering through their sixth straight year of drought. A half-million men, women, and children were already dead and an estimated 10 million more were living at near starvation levels throughout the North African famine belt.

Although some rain did finally arrive later in the decade, all the horrifying scenes (only worse) were to be repeated by the mid-1980s. Thus did the developed world get their first close-up coverage of the grim realities of mass starvation. We could no longer ignore the suffering as the catastrophe was simply too large.

Of course, these crises would pass as had many others for centuries before them. Yet the uneasy feeling around the world could not be forgotten as leaders discussed the possibility of an eventual famine affecting not just millions, but billions of people in the low income countries of the world.

There is no doubt that Americans will have enough food for many years to come. Even under the worst conditions those in the "over-developed" countries will probably continue to eat luxuriously[41] and even to feed protein-rich food to pets. We have the income; we can therefore generate effective demand.

But what about the approximately 3 billion people in the less developed or Third World countries? What will become of them? What are their chances for survival? The problem of mass poverty must be considered *the* major economic issue of our time.

The regions under consideration include Asia (except Japan and Taiwan), Black Africa, and Latin America. Although some of these countries are better off than others, we are essentially talking about two-thirds of the world's population. Let's now take a moment to examine some of the general characteristics that are common to many of these Third World countries.

Certainly one common element in most low-income countries is the problem of *mass illiteracy*. Scarce resources often go toward the education of elite classes who are taught an outmoded colonial type of curriculum in schools which deemphasize the skills needed for economic development. For prestigious reasons, students often choose "literate" professions or civil service training instead of business, farming, trades, or engineering, moving into a world of bureaucratic desks and white shirts rather than to one of farms or factories.

Other students come to the United States, England, or France to receive legal training or to become doctors, eventually to serve an upper-class clientele. Some never return to their homeland. Not only does this kind of training use up scarce public money that could be used for adult literacy classes or paramedical training, but it also tends to reinforce class consciousness and widen income differentials.

Nutrition is also often a problem. Even without famine conditions, poor countries have always had difficulty obtaining food with adequate protein.

Protein deficiency, in turn, may eventually result in the crippling disease known as *kwashiorkor*. The victims are almost always children, seen in photographs with their large, protruding bellies and thin, reddish hair. Another nutritional disease is *zerophthalmia*, which comes about from a deficiency in vitamin A. This deficiency exposes millions to a bacterial eye infection that can lead to permanent blindness. In addition, there are many other nutritional diseases that in one way or another impair mental and physical performance.

Do these nutritional problems mean that the industrialized countries ought to supply poor countries with free food? Such generosity would, ironically, probably do more harm than good (at least in the long run) *by obstructing the evolution of their own agricultural industries.*

To illustrate this point, imagine the impact if some "benevolent" country gave free milk to everyone in the United States. In a short period of time much of the U.S. dairy industry would be forced into bankruptcy. Soon we would all be unnecessarily dependent on the charity of this "benevolent" country.

No, what the Third World farmer needs is really no different from what other successful farmers need in order to be productive; i.e., *good economic incentives* such as reasonably high and stable commodity prices, access to land, credit, marketing cooperatives, and appropriate farm technology.[42] Frequently, a successful agricultural industry can get under way by simply *eliminating obstacles* that already exist including elitist land-tenure arrangements or artificially low prices imposed by the government to placate urban workers. Indeed, a successful agrarian base is often the best method of providing food to the masses and thus upgrading nutritional levels.

Also, Third World countries generally lack *productive capital,* which would include among other things, productive tools, machines, and factories. Indeed, the average African or Asian peasant does use a certain amount of low-level capital goods—hoes, wooden plows, hand manufacturing tools, etc. But these are extremely unproductive.

The key word here is *productivity.* The growth process in the capital-intensive countries goes something like this: First, highly productive labor generates a large amount of output, which translates into relatively high incomes for workers. High wage rates, though, mean increasing costs to the producer; producers, therefore, are forced to mechanize even more, which again increases productivity. The growth sequence thus begins another round.

On the other hand, the less developed country cannot generate high incomes because of the extremely low productivity of its capital resources. What we find is the "vicious circle of underdevelopment"—low productivity, low incomes, and a low level of consumption. The overall productivity in most poor countries is so low that a large percentage of the people live at the subsistence level, producing so little that they are forced to exist just barely above the survival line.

Indeed, it is this living near the margin of survival without prospect of upward mobility that distinguishes the "living poor" of the Third World countries from the poor of the industrialized countries:

> Living poor is like being sentenced to exist in a stormy sea in a battered canoe, requiring all your strength simply to keep afloat; there is never any question of reaching a destination. True poverty is a state of perpetual crisis, and one wave just a little bigger or coming from an unexpected direction can and usually does wreck things. Some benevolent ignorance denies a poor man the ability to see the squalid sequence of his life, except very rarely; he views it rather as a disconnected string of unfortunate sadnesses. Never having paddled on a calm sea, he is unable to imagine one. I think if he could connect the chronic hunger, the sickness, the death of his children, the almost unrelieved physical and emotional tension into the pattern that his life inevitably takes, he would kill himself.[43]

Thus, the poor in the developing countries live with uncertainty, substandard living conditions, illiteracy, poor health, and hunger, all combined with a traditional economic system based on unskilled labor and low-productivity tools.

There is, however, another element of underdevelopment that is not as visible as those described above, an element that may be even more harmful to development efforts than the lack of productive resources. This is an area economists call *institutional barriers to change*, which includes adverse power relationships, elitist political systems, cultural traditions, tribalism, graft and corruption, and the impact of foreign values. Relevant questions pertaining to institutional problems might include:

- How do traditional cultural practices affect development efforts?
- How equal or unequal is the distribution of wealth and income?
- What percentage of those engaged in agriculture are landless?
- What role do foreign values or economic interests play in indigenous development? How conducive are conditions for import replacement?

Rick Graefe

- How strong is the national feeling? How loyal are the citizens to the state, its laws, and its planning requirements (vs. narrow "tribal" or religious loyalties)?

Let's begin with the question of traditional culture and its effect on economic development. Many economists feel that the major obstacle to economic betterment is the simple desire to have a large family. In almost every underdeveloped country we find great status (as well as future "social security") given to parents who have many surviving children. Yet such a simple cultural value can create monumental social and economic problems. A 2 percent population growth rate, for example, can result in the doubling of a population in about thirty-five years. Although some Third World countries greatly exceed that 2 percent figure, the world as a whole averages out to about 1.7 percent. Still, this means that there will be over 6 billion people by the year 2000—up from today's approximate 5 billion figure. Most of the net increase will, of course, be in the poorest regions of the world.

The above numbers may mean more when they are put into historical perspective. For example, it took about 2 million years of human history to bring our world population up to its first billion people. The second billion were added in about a hundred years. The third billion took only thirty years, and the fourth took but fifteen years. Now if the 1.7 percent population growth rate figures holds, we will have approximately 8 billion by the year 2015, and 16 billion only a generation later (2055)! Again, most of these increases would be added to the populations of the less developed countries.

These figures are indeed staggering. Such large numbers will undoubtedly be modified either by increasing overall death rates or, more humanely, by declining birth rates. Indeed, population experts have pointed out that much more could be done in the area of birth control and family planning. It is interesting to note that the most successful countries along this line are either authoritarian (mainland China, for example) or have at one time demonstrated rapid economic growth such as Taiwan, Singapore, and Hong Kong. Ironically, the best and least repressive method to reverse people's attitudes about family size is through economic development—helping children survive through better health measures and, perhaps most important, providing outside work opportunities for women. Indeed, after years of traveling, researching, and evaluating family planning programs, writer Pranay Gupta, in his book *The Crowded Earth*, put the greatest emphasis on the importance of upgrading the economic status of women:

> I found during my travels that more and more women also seem to want to get out of their homes to involve themselves in economic activities, a situation that could eventually lead to even more women producing fewer children and thus bring down Asian nations' annual population growth rates. The experience of places such as Bali, Sri Lanka, South Korea, and the southern Indian state of Kerela has shown that, where women were brought into the economic mainstream through increased female education and employment, there was not only an overall decline in the population growth rate but also an improvement in the content and pace of development and in the general quality of life of the entire community.[44]

Yet for many of the very poorest Third World countries, economic opportunities, health care resources, and other fruits of economic development are often beyond the reach of individuals, families, and communities caught in the vicious circle of poverty. On the one hand, high population growth rates stifle economic development potential; on the other hand, women will want fewer children only if they have access to greater opportunities and see that there is a high probability that their children will survive. Can anything be done about this dilemma?

Perhaps one answer is economic assistance from the developed countries. But it should not be the usual type of aid that finances impressive capital-intensive projects such as dams, airports, international hotels, etc. Instead, it should be financial or technical assistance for local projects that promote widespread benefits in nutrition, health, education, clean water, housing, small-scale rural technologies, and, where it is requested, assistance in family planning projects. It's doubtful whether these "people-oriented" investments will increase the gross national product as much as a new steel mill or hydroelectric plant. But a more equal distribution of income and the possibility of reducing fertility rates may well be far more beneficial in the long run.

Consider too another major problem for Thirld World development, i.e., the *uneven concentration of power, wealth, and income.* To understand the distribution of wealth and power in the poor countries, we must first grasp the importance of land. Poor countries are usually agrarian societies in which more than three quarters of the population work and live in rural areas (compared with 5 percent, for example, in the United States). In such communities prestige, wealth, and power are measured not so much by capital, money, or material goods but by the amount of land one controls. Think, for example, of the Philippines, a country that has shown some economic growth but little widespread development, where well over half of those working in agriculture are landless. We could also journey to Latin America where the magnificent estates, tens of thousands of acres, are owned by just a few families; to Venezuela where 1 percent of the landowners own more than half of the total land; or to El Salvador where 2 percent of the wealthiest families own about half of the best farmland. We could also find many great plantations extending for miles throughout fertile regions of Africa and Asia.

These vast acreages and plantations produce tremendous riches for the owners but usually mean continued poverty and dependence for the workers or renters:

> In South America the poor man is an ignorant man, unaware of the forces that shape his destiny. The shattering truth—that he is kept poor and ignorant as the principal and unspoken component of national policy—escapes him. He cries for land reform, a system of farm loans that will carry him along between crops, unaware that the national economy in almost every country sustained by a one-crop export commodity depends for its success on an unlimited supply of cheap labor. Ecuador needs poor men to compete in the world banana market; Brazil needs poverty to sell its coffee, and so on.[45]

Concentrated wealth, however, is not limited to local landlords and the traditional elite classes. Some foreigners, particularly those who "stayed behind" from the former colonies, also own immense parcels of property. Also, foreign interests frequently dominate the mining sectors that extract large amounts of raw materials from beneath the earth's surface—tin from Bolivia, petroleum from Nigeria and Mexico, copper from Zambia and Chile, aluminum ore from Guinea. The list of foreign investments is extensive, and while such investments may bring some employment advantages, the long-run benefits to the poor are questionable when one considers the exported profits, the continued dependency, the strains created by unequal growth, and the tremendous reliance on one or two exports to earn foreign exchange.

This last point takes on even greater significance when we learn that about half of the foreign exchange for a sizable group of developing countries was earned by the export of just one or two raw materials. This means, for example, that Bolivia's ability to purchase imports (capital goods, food, consumer products, etc.) is largely dependent on how much foreign exchange can be earned exporting tin. Under these conditions, a small drop in tin prices could bring tremendous financial problems. Foreign exchange earnings would drop significantly, consumption of imports would be curtailed, the balance of payments would take a turn for the worse, and major development projects might have to be cut back—all this from a relatively small drop in the price of tin.

Manufacturing industries are frequently dominated by foreign interests too. Indeed, our journey to typical Third World countries would not be complete until we visited the industrial parks on the fringes of the major capitals. Here, Westerners would feel much at home with the familiar corporations—Coca Cola, Ford, Union Carbide, and Texaco, not to mention branch factories of British, German, French, and Dutch firms. These multinational corporations manufacture everything from soap, shoes, and ballpoint pens to bicycles and portable radios. Native manufacturing, in turn, may be stifled as the small scale of local operations usually cannot compete with giant foreign companies.

Given the lopsided distribution of wealth and the dominance of foreign interests, there may be little incentive for local economic development. Why build up a rural homestead if you don't own the land and can't benefit from your labors? Why attempt to compete with the giant companies when you are at a disadvantage in all phases of operation, from obtaining raw materials to marketing the product? In summary, institutional barriers can be quite deadening to economic incentives.

So what can be done about institutional problems? Some economists believe that it is necessary to have powerful governments that, over time, can force the necessary reforms and remove the obstacles to economic betterment. The centralized authorities must have the means and the will to radically alter land-tenure relationships, to reduce the enormous inequalities, and to evolve an effective program of population control combined with mass health and hygienic improvements.

Governments must also facilitate the emergence of local entrepreneurs and create economic environments, particularly around cities, conducive to the critical process of import-replacing.[46] They must encourage national savings so there is financial capital available for business loans and essential public services. But equally important, they need to safeguard traditional communities that seek economic self-reliance via their own traditional ways. They must learn to recognize when it is better to keep out of economic affairs and when it is correct to step in.

Indeed, these are difficult tasks for the world's young nation states. Many poor countries presently lack a sense of national legitimacy, unity, and long-term stability needed to institute such changes. In some countries democratic reforms may not be enough. Thus, we should not be surprised to see the rise of authoritarian regimes. Many will be corrupt and antithetical to widespread development efforts; but others will undoubtedly evolve the right mix of democracy, intervention, and encouragement of independent action. Indeed, we are bound to witness an era that is certain to have great strife and suffering. Still the prospects are immense:

> Yet if the Great Ascent is slow, cruel, even fearsome, it is also irresistible, stirring, grandiose. It is an avenue of history which, however difficult, leads from an eternity of dark suffering toward the possibility of light and life. That it will surely usher in a period of disorder, readjustment, even temporary defeat is as true for the fortunate few as for the unfortunate many, but it is also possible to see such a period as prelude to a more distant era in which, for the first time, the potentialities of the entire human race may be explored.[47]

Thus, one of the major problems in economics today is how we, in the highly developed countries, can help bring about the necessary changes in the poorest countries. Only by our under-standing, by our sharing of resources and technical know how, and by our willingness to make some sacrifices, can we someday hope to reduce the world's gross economic imbalances. This is the challenge facing us all.

NOTES

1. See, for example Bernd Herinrich's book *Bumblebee Economics* (Harvard, 1979) where the author examines the bumblebee's economic problem primarily in terms of energy efficiency. Another related book is Donald Worster's *Nature's Economy* (Anchor, 1979), his title derived from the early naturalist's concept of what is today called "ecology." Note the word "ecology" has the same root as the word "economics": *oikos* (Greek for household). Thus the natural world also has cooperation, competition, inputs and outputs, maximizations, etc., as nature attempts to maintain its "household." Its "management" is not a matter of consciously choosing alternatives (as we do) but is primarily genetic, adaptive, and evolutionary. Incidently, Darwin's great insight of natural selection came to him while reading the great 18th Century economists including Adam Smith and even more importantly, Thomas Malthus, whose essay *On Population* led Darwin to the idea of nature's "struggle for existence." (see *Charles Darwin's Autobiography*, Henry Schuman, 1950, p. 54)

2. See Vernon Carter and Tom Dale, *Topsoil and Civilization*, (Norman, OK: University of Oklahoma Press, 1974). This is perhaps the best reference I have seen that puts the depletion of the world's topsoil in a historical context.

3. See, for example how this conditioning takes place in children's literature in *Dick & Jane as Victims—Sex Stereotyping in Childrens' Readers* (Princeton, NJ: Women on Words and Images, 1975.)

4. Robert L. Heilbroner, *The Making of Economic Society*, (Englewood Cliffs, NJ: Prentice-Hall, 1962), p. 15.

5. See any issue of *The Mother Earth News* (Hendersonville, North Carolina).

6. North Country Anvil, #4 (Box 37, Millville, MN 55957).

7. George B. Leonard, "Winning Isn't Everything, It's Nothing," *Intellectual Digest* (1973): 47.

8. Milton Friedman, "The Voucher Idea," *New York Times Magazine* (1973): 23. See also John Coons and Stephen Sugarman, *Education by Choice: The Case for Family Control* (Berkeley, CA: University of California Press, 1978). In a modification of the public school voucher idea, Harvard economist Lester Thurow has proposed a "skill voucher" for those who do not choose to go to college. Thurow suggests such a voucher would be

worth $12,000 or an amount equal to the average subsidy currently received by college students. (see *The Zero Sum Solution,* p. 205, Simon &. Schuster, 1985)

9. Maurice Zeitlin, ed., *American Society, Inc.,* (Chicago: Markham Publishing Co., 1970), pp. 513–514.

10. From *The Retreat From Riches* by Peter Passell and Leonard Ross, (New York: Viking Press, New York: 1971), p. 36.

11. George F. Will, "Unpadding the 'Padded Society,'" *Newsweek* (1981): 100.

12. The attempts to increase productivity in some professions—high-speed drills for dentists, clinics for doctors, TV courses for educators—have undoubtedly kept costs and prices from rising higher than they would have without the productivity gain.

13. See Milton Friedman, *Capitalism and Freedom* (Chicago: University of Chicago Press, 1962), p. 150. In his chapter "Occupational Licensure" Friedman suggests that all professional licensing (including medical licensing) should be abolished in favor of a more free entry into the occupations. According to Friedman, this would ultimately lower the cost of professional services for the consumer.

14. For more details on Ehrlich's analyses and predictions, see Paul Ehrlich and Ann Ehrlich, *Extinction* (New York: Random House, 1981).

15. Arthur Schlesinger, Jr., "Neo-Conservatism and the Class Struggle," *Wall Street Journal* (1981).

16. See William Lowrance, *Of Acceptable Risk: Science and the Determination of Safety* (Los Altos, CA: Kaufmann, 1976). This book provides a detailed discussion of how our government views the nature of consumer and worker risks as related to costs and benefits.

17. Saul Pett, "The Bloated Bureaucracy," *St. Paul Pioneer Press* (1981): 4.

18. See *The Eight Myths of Poverty,* by William O'Hare, *American Demographics,* May 1986, p. 24.

19. This data was taken from Greg Duncan's book, *Years of Poverty, Years of Plenty* (Institute for Social Research, Ann Arbor, 1984.)

20. Op. cit. (O'Hare) p. 25

21. Michael Harrington, *The Other America* (New York: Macmillan, 1962), p. 13.

22. Simone de Beauvoir, *The Coming of Age* (New York: Warner Books, 1971), p. 690.

23. See Michael Harrington's more recent book, *The New American Poverty* (Holt, Rinehart & Winston (1984), p. 690.

24. See footnote 8.

25. See Scott Burns, *The Household Economy* (Boston: Beacon Press, 1977). If you are interested in learning more about the hidden productive capabilities of the household sector, I highly recommend this text. In addition, Burns has done some interesting work in calculating a "rate of return" for home-production-type investments, which he claims compare very favorably with corporate-type investments. In Scott Burns, "The Economics of Milling Your Own Flour," *Organic Gardening and Farming* (1976): 103. Burns estimated that the rate of return to the homeowner for an electric grain mill was around 40 percent—over three times the return from the average corporate investment.

26. Leopold Kohr, *Overdeveloped Nations* (New York: Schocken Books, 1978), p. 39.

27. Wade Green and Soma Golden, "Luddites Were not all Wrong," *New York Times Magazine.* The most extreme position I have seen concerning economic growth and man's ecological destructiveness is in the poetry by the late California poet Robinson Jeffers. Many readers have interpreted his poetry to essentially say that "the human race is, in fact, not needed." See Gilbert Highet, *The Powers of Poetry* (New York: Oxford University Press, 1960), pp. 133–134.

28. Irving Kristol, "The Worst is Yet to Come," *Wall Street Journal* (Nov. 26, 1979, p. 24).

29. Mel Ellis, "The Good Earth," *Milwaukee Journal* (1974):

30. E. B. White, *The Points of My Compass* (New York: Harper & Row, 1962), p. 67.

31. Henry Caudill, *My Land Is Dying* (New York: Dutton, 1971), p. 104.

32. *The Quality of Life;* James A. Michener (Lippincott, 1970, p. 86–87).

33. *The Making of the President, 1964;* Theodore H. White (Atheneum, 1965) p. 322.

34. The highly respected forecasting newsletter, *Blue Chip Economic Indicators* (which uses a "consensus" approach of averaging the projections from approximately 50 economists), projected in March 1982 an

inflation rate of 6.9% for '83, 6.6% in '84, and 6.4% for '85. In contrast, the actual rates (GNP Price Deflator) was 3.8% in '83, 4.1% in '84, and only 3.3% in '85. (Sources: *Blue Chip Economic Indicators,* Sedona, AZ, March 10, 1982, p. 7, and *The Economic Report of the President,* Feb. 1986, Washington, D.C., p. 257.)

35. See John Galbraith, *The Great Crash* (Boston: Houghton Mifflin, 1961) for a fascinating account of 1929's "Black Tuesday" and the early days of the depression.

36. James R. Adams, "Supply-Side Roots of the Founding Fathers," *Wall Street Journal* (1981): (Nov. 17, 1981, p. 26)

37. For an entertaining view of the economic history of money (including an interesting commentary on money's psychological importance) see Henry Lindgren's book, *Great Expectations* (William Kaufmann, 1980).

38. Walter W. Haines, *Money, Prices, and Policy* (New York: McGraw-Hill, 1958) pp. 24–25.

39. Quoted from *The Arizona Republic,* Jan. 4, 1986, p. 1E.

40. "Angry Workers Desecrate Flag in Milwaukee," *St. Paul Pioneer Press* (1981): 1.

41. See Frances Moore Lappe, *Diet for a Small Planet* (New York: Ballantine Books, 1975).

42. It should be noted that a growing number of economists are concerned that the less developed countries are adopting large-scale technology. This is happening because they want to emulate developed countries' production techniques, and because middle or "intermediate" technology is simply not available. One economist who not only described the problem but also started "intermediate technology groups" to develop tools and equipment more suited for poor, labor-intensive countries is the late E. F. Schumacher. See E. F. Schumacher, *Small Is Beautiful* and the follow-up book, George McRobie, *Small Is Possible* (New York: Harper & Row, 1981).

43. Mortz Thomsen, *Living Poor: A Peace Corps Chronicle* (University of Washington Press, 1969).

44. *The Crowded Earth,* Pranay Gupta (Norton 1984): p. 109.

45. Op. cit. (Thomsen) p. 173.

46. For an innovative analysis on the importance of cities and the process of important substitution, see Jane Jacob's book, *Cities and the Wealth of Nations* (Random, 1984).

47. Robert Heilbroner, *The Great Ascent* (New York: Harper & Row, 1963), p. 158.

INDEX